YOUR CALL IS IMPORTANT TO US

YOUR CALL IS IMPORTANT TO US

The Truth About BULLSHIT

LAURA PENNY

CROWN PUBLISHERS
NEW YORK

ISBN 0-7394-6448-5

Printed in the United States of America

Title page photograph copyright © Peter Dazeley/CORBIS

For my family

Acknowledgments

I have many people to thank for this, and the first is Gary Ross. This book was his idea, and he shepherded me through the early stages of its production. I'd also like to thank the rest of the staff at the now-defunct MacFarlane, Walter, and Ross. I am very grateful to McClelland and Stewart for picking up the manuscript after MWR's unfortunate demise, and extend special thanks to Marilyn Biderman and Dinah Forbes at McClelland. I'd also like to thank Crown, my American publisher, and my editor there, Rachel Klayman.

I am also profoundly grateful to all the policy wonks, journalists, authors, and experts cited in my notes for doing the good work, and providing me with hours—nay, years—of enlightenment and entertainment.

Those are some of the nice people who helped me make the book, and I extend a blanket thanks to all the others who made this book pretty and available. I'd also like to thank the people who make me me. First, thanks to Sarah Fulford, for many years of friendship and support. Thanks to my mom and dad for reading many drafts. Thanks to the people who helped me goof off and not think about the book, like the brothers Forbes, Rosa Alcala, and kim dawn. Thanks to my teachers, in particular, Harold Kyte, Dr. Elizabeth Edwards, Dr. Calin Mihailescu, and Dr. Rodolphe Gasché. Thanks to my delightful colleagues and students at the University of King's College in Halifax, Nova Scotia.

Finally, last but not least, thanks to C.B., for everything, every day.

Contents

YOUR CALL IS IMPORTANT TO US

CHAPTER ONE

YOU'RE SOAKING IN IT

*No matter how cynical you become, it is never enough to
keep up.*

—LILY TOMLIN

We live in an era of unprecedented bullshit production.
The more polite among you might call it poppycock or
balderdash or claptrap, but the concept remains the same, and
the same coursing stream of crapulence washes over us all, fill-
ing our eyes and ears and thoughts with clichés, euphemisms,
evasions, and fabulations. Never in the history of mankind
have so many people uttered statements that they know to be
untrue. Presidents, priests, politicians, lawyers, reporters, corporate executives, and countless others have taken to saying
not what they actually believe, but what they want others to
believe—not what is, but what works.

I am not so naive as to lay claim to some golden age when
everybody meant what they said, and said what they meant,
and the world entire was bright with the glare of truth. First, I
came to consciousness in the eighties, so people have been
conducting themselves in a sleazy manner the whole of my

short life. Second, every historical era conjures up its own lies, noble and banal. Since there have been snakes for the squeezing, there has been someone to flog their precious oil. We distinguish ourselves largely in terms of largeness. Our era is unique by virtue of its sheer scale, its massive budget, its seemingly unlimited capability to send bullshit hurtling rapidly over the globe.

There is so much bullshit that one hardly knows where to begin. The platitudinous pabulum that passes for stirring political rhetoric is bullshit. The scripted, question-proof events that pretend to be spontaneous exchanges are bullshit. The committee-crafted persona and the focus-grouped fad and the rule of the polls are straight-up bullshit. The disease hysteria du jour is bullshit, and so is the latest miracle pill. The new product that will change your life is probably just more cheap, plastic bullshit. We endure bullshit in the course of our workaday lives, in the form of management-speak memos about optimizing strategic objectives and result-based, value-added service delivery. We tolerate bullshit in common life-maintenance transactions, like banking and shopping. Most of what passes for news is bullshit, and even if you are so fortunate as to find things worth watching or reading, the content you desire will be punctuated with shills for things you don't need, like ginormous automobiles and toxic faux foodstuffs.

Even a cursory study of bullshit yields an embarrassment of riches, an all-you-can-eat buffet of phoniness, like when a Bush staffer eulogizes departing press secretary Ari Fleischer with the words, "His message discipline was extraordinary," a bullshit description of a peerless bullshitter. Or check out the Web presence of a swank PR firm, like Burson-Marsteller, mouthpieces for many a megacorp, and thrill to their proficiency in *change communications, issues management, reputa-*

tion management, and the coup de grâce, *personal and social responsibility.*

"Your call is important to us" has been chosen from a very deep reservoir of bullshit phrases for the title of this book because it best exemplifies the properties native to bullshit. It tries to slather some nice on the result of a simple ratio: your time versus some company's dough. Like most bullshit, the more times you hear it, the bullshittier it gets. This is why bullshit is best served quickly, with many visuals, in mass quantities, with no questions from the floor.

Throughout this book, we will look at some of the world's muchness of bullshit. I have elected to proceed on a sector-by-sector basis, since bullshit is not just a phenomenon but an industry—one of the growth industries of the information age, in fact. But bullshit is not a single industry unto itself, nor a sector proper. Instead, it rides shotgun, running interference for all the major modern sectors. We shall commence by looking at the two fields of human endeavor that have distinguished themselves as the most prolific producers of bullshit: advertising and public relations, which get bonus points for encouraging the industries that follow in their wake to tart themselves up. Next, we will see how financial markets, corporate structures, and lax laws allow for more merde, with entire companies—your Enrons, your WorldComs—exposed as mortared with bullshit. Then we'll have a look at politics, which is a business as well, alas. Finally, we'll look at a few examples of bullshit produced by some of the sectors that affect your everyday life, like pharmaceuticals, insurance, the service industry, and the media.

We are all, of course, implicated in the bullshit pandemic as minor, small-scale producers of our own ordure. I would love to be hard-core like my favorite Enlightenment philosopher, Immanuel Kant, and declare that all lies are wrong, and that there are no circumstances whatsoever that condone untruth. Kant thought that any lie, no matter how minor or well-intentioned, corrodes the universality and trust that people need to live freely, and I couldn't agree more. But I'd be lying if I said I never lied, and I'm sure you could conjure a million retarded Philosophy 101 variations on the theme of virtuous fibs. It is therefore crucial to note that there are very different orders of magnitude when it comes to bullshit.

Those couple of daily white lies, about bad haircuts and spousal girth and the like, are entirely harmless and preferable to the useless, hurtful truth. Good manners sometimes call for omission, editing, and the occasional fudge. However, if your secretary is shredding documents by the light of the moon, or your testimony before the House interrupts the soaps, or you have yet to visit the country where all your money lives, you have probably concocted a whopper of inordinate size.

Nor am I unduly concerned with the gap between appearance and reality with respect to the way the common man woos his wife, greets his co-workers, or combs his hair. It takes millions and millions of dollars, and a solid toehold in the public consciousness, to prick up my ears. When something installs itself in popular culture, that is when I begin to wonder about the gaps between what that thing does, says, and says about what it does. If I fault the spectacularly wealthy and powerful the more for embroidering the truth, it is not because they bullshit more frequently than their lunchmeat-munching lessers, but simply because they get a lot more out of it, thus setting a very bad example that ensures continued bullshitting all the way down the line. Dollars may not trickle down, but lessons and images certainly do.

I am even tempted to make the case that lying is less dangerous than bullshitting. In his essay "On Bullshit," professor Harry Frankfurt draws a subtle and useful distinction between lying and bullshitting. The liar still cares about the truth. The bullshitter is unburdened by such concerns. Bullshit-related phrases like *bull session* or *talking shit* also suggest a casual, careless attitude toward veracity—a sense that the truth is totally beside the point. Bullshit distracts with exaggeration, omission, obfuscation, stock phrases, pretentious jargon, faux-folksiness, feigned ignorance, and sloganeering homilies. When Dubya speaks of freedom and liberation, and claims to be praying for peace as the army disgorges load after load of bombs, he is not lying. He is bullshitting. A lie would be a simpler, more factual thing, like, nope, we aren't dropping any bombs. A lie would be easier to disprove. Bullshit is a committee-drafted simpleton's sermon about evildoers and terra and freedom being God's gift to all men.

This is bullshit because it tricks out a terrible thing in floaty, fulsome rhetoric. Bullshit is forever putting the rosiest of spins on rotten political and economic decisions. This is because bullshit is all about getting away with something, or getting someone to buy something in the broadest possible sense, which means covering arses or kissing them. Bullshit is always trying to be your buddy, getting all chummy with you, making greasy nice. Nobody passes a bill because they got a bale of cash from some industry concern; instead, they wax poetic about the good people of Any District who will benefit immensely from the new legislation. Nobody leaves office because they fucked up; no, they want to spend more time with their families. No mogul says I do it all for the money, suckers. They blah-dee-blah on about the company, or some magnificent abstract idea the company embodies.

Bullshit aggrandizes and amplifies. Sometimes this is a sign of the bullshitter's luxuriant self-regard, like when athletes or actresses praise the original G for their achievements. This is supposed to make the star in question seem humble as well as Christian, which is a very popular bullshit pose, particularly among the obscenely wealthy. Instead of striking a modest note, though, such statements imply that the supreme being has the time, inclination, and interest to fix the Oscars or the Super Bowl. Though the famous contribute plenty of name-brand bullshit to the culture, bullshit is more often produced anonymously. It tends to be cranked out by hacks and flacks, in the interest of aggrandizing and amplifying the object it is slathered all over, whether that's a celebrity, a product, a candidate, a disease, a war, a service, or an event.

Bullshit is not just happy talk. There are also bullshit scares and threats that hold the public in a thrall of fear, all the while eclipsing many genuinely problematic international developments. Prime-time newsmagazines like *Dateline* and *20/20* excel at uncovering the latest lurid crime or horror at home, airing gross buckets of alarmist bullshit about satanic nannies and con-artist plumbers. Cable networks shine when it comes to puffing up minor hobgoblins into major panics, like shark attacks or the Summer of SARS, and making made-for-TV miniseries like the one on the Laci Peterson case, and *Saving Private Jessica,* the book, the movie, and the centcom agitprop.

Bullshit also minimizes, making sure the proverbial buck never, ever stops. Such bullshit includes the fetid apologies of irresponsible corporations and unaccountable politicians, the excuse-making and name-changing that follow any mistake or massacre. Examples of this include Phillip Morris christening itself Altria, Enron restructuring itself into the utterly generic InternationalCo, and Dow's self-flagellating Bhopal website, which, amid the mea culpas, underlines the fact that they assume no legal liability for the misadventures of their offending subsidiary, Union Carbide.

One of the really fascinating things about bullshit is how utterly obvious a lot of it is. When one of the Enron dudes takes the stand and pleads the fifth or uses weasel phrases like "I cannot recall," he is not lying. He is bullshitting. He is bullshitting because the whole routine is so flagrantly false that it sails gaily past traditional notions of deception. It's not like he expects us to believe that early onset Alzheimer's has rendered that whole making-millions-of-dollars thing, like, a total blur. It is not a lame excuse or limp self-justification. Dude is not even trying. He is merely repeating the legally appropriate, self-protecting thing one says on such occasions, giving voice to the typical script.

Most people believe that they can recognize the typical script as such, and consider themselves excellent bullshit detectors. Bullshit detection is the stuff of which modern social bonds are made. We huddle in little clusters, or gather on the Web, rolling our eyes in unison, bitching and moaning about the bullshit. We praise the superior interpretative skills of our respective social sets and marvel at the terminally credulous cretins, somewhere out there, who are actually swallowing this bilge. And we talk this way whether we are discussing politics or pop culture. The fact that most of us feel like we can see through the prevailing pretenses but expect and accept them is part and parcel of the way bullshit works. Bullshit thrives on the soft bigotry of low expectations.

Cynicism, irony, and apathy—the ostensible markers of Gen Xers like me—are often dismissed by elder virtuecrats as a lack of good old-fashioned values. This virtuecratic stance may be more commonly associated with conservative politicians, but Democrats like Al Gore and Joe Lieberman have also been quick to pick on the usual pop-culture objects of blame, like video games, TV, movies, and rap music. When the banner of godliness is held aloft by hypocrites like William Bennett, who blew millions in Vegas even as he cranked out book after book of virtues, or Newt Gingrich, who talked family values but divorced his own wife in the midst of her terminal illness, it casts doubt on the very idea of a moral high ground.

Cynicism and apathy are, in fact, reasonable responses to the refulgent tide of bullshit in which we have bobbed all our lives. We have seen too many hopeful Reaganisms like "It's morning in America" give way to scandals like Iran-Contra. One of the reasons why people—particularly the young—are opting out of old-school civic duties like voting and reading the newspaper is that they are weary of bullshit.

It would be overstating the case, though, to claim that this apathy is a form of conscientious objection. Apathy is also a consequence of being, like, sooo totally distracted. There is a lot of other bullshit that is way more entertaining than the yawny old newspaper. North Americans live at the intersection of too much and too little information—a great location for bullshit production, since bullshit often begins with some little smidge of truth, like the hearsay headline or the overheard opinion. The bullshitter knows a little something, or thinks that he does, and rather than admit ignorance, soldiers bravely on. All of us, save for the most scrupulous, have doubtless blithered our way through a conversation regarding matters we do not know much about, like talking about "unrest"—a classic bullshit euphemism—in a place we couldn't point to on a map.

But too much information is no antidote to too little of it, since so much of this information is strictly commercial, ephemeral, or shorn of context. This semi-knowledge annexes valuable public and mental space, as do all the things not worth knowing that you can't not know, try though you may to avoid the *Matrix* sequels or the latest Britney Spears release.

There are several different dialects of bullshit, indigenous to various institutions and professions. We will look at these later, in detail, when we encounter the bizarre lingua francas of specific industries. But now I would like to draw a more basic distinction between the two major types of bullshit: the complex and the simple. Complex bullshit is also known as bafflegab or jargon, and it is the native argot of modern bureaucracy. Simple bullshit is all about the dumbed-down, the quick hit, the ad, or the blip on the cable news crawl. Most information in North America seems to come in one of two settings: Expert or Moron. Expert is the lengthy contract you sign to get a loan or mortgage from a bank, and Moron is the brightly colored brochure that encouraged you to bank at the First National House of Usury. Expert is the snarl of subsidiaries and tax dodges established by Enron with the help of Arthur Andersen's finest; Moron is Ken Lay and the gang putting on a happy face and maintaining that all is well.

Complex bullshit is full of feats of abstract reasoning that would astonish a medieval theologian. An infinity of holding companies can be set to dance upon the head of the slenderest offshore pin. Even business types have become alarmed by their own flights of jargoneering. In 2003, Deloitte & Touche released a new software program called Bullfighter, which flags offending terms like *synergy, incentivize,* and *paradigm*. Deloitte's consultants argued that this sort of obfuscating bafflegab is a bad sign, business-model-wise, citing examples like the Internet bubble, when people invested gobs of spondulicks in business plans they did not understand. These plans sounded pretty fantastic, but were categorically un-understandable because they made no sense, and were not in the pedestrian business of sense-making. Anyone can make sense. Only the revolutionary few can make millions by incentivizing synergy paradigms.

Bafflegab is not written to explain. It is written to impress and confound, and it is by no means confined to the business world, although that is where it thrives. The government also cranks out documents that impress and confound with their sheer bulk and impenetrability. Curl up with your tax code, or the North American Free Trade Agreement. Marvel at its dogged reader-resistance, the clauses of legalese and the confusing constructions. Whether you read them or not, these bricks of bafflegab determine the quality of your life. The boring is where they keep the consequences.

Simple bullshit does not demand decoding. We flee to the cozy no-think of simple bullshit after furrowing our brows at the complex stuff. It is all pretty colors and easy fixes and exactly what you want to hear. It should be fairly obvious by this point that bullshits simple and complex are Siamese twins of a sort, with simple running interference and serving as the smiling public face of complex bullshit. Simple bullshit is pitched to the lowest common denominator, and is not just stupid, but actively stupefying. One of the most important things I have learned from teaching is that the presumption of stupidity leads to the production of stupidity. Simple bullshit doesn't just lower the public discourse bar. It buries it deep in the cold, cold ground.

Simple bullshit is generally too good to be true, telling you that everything is okay, that you are loved, that you are number one, that you deserve a break today, that the solution to all your problems is but a product or ideology away. Bullshit simple comes on strong and cloying, like the cheating boyfriend who buys too many bouquets. Simple bullshit is not all sweetness and light, though. Simple bullshit also demonizes. Bullshit simple is the tongue of political demagogues left and right, be they fundie hymn-belting creeps like John Ashcroft, covering the nipples on statues, or charmless virtuecrats like Al Gore and Joe Lieberman, condemning video games they have never played. The gossip, trash talk, bullying, and closed-minded combativeness that pass for contemporary political coverage and commentary are good examples of simple bullshit, the best-selling representatives being the eminent belligerents Rush Limbaugh, Bill O'Reilly, and Ann Coulter.

We certainly cannot take credit for inventing bullshit: You can go all the way back to ancient Egypt and find texts bemoaning the fact that everyone lies. But we have made it—to use a few of our favorite adjectives—bolder, brighter, bigger, better, stronger, faster. We have supersized it. No previous cluster of imperial or religious bullshit-production apparatuses has grown as huge, efficient, and well funded as rapidly, or dispersed itself over the face of the globe in quite the way ours has. Part of this is a consequence of technological innovations like radio, television, and computers, which provide brand-new outlets and unprecedented audiences for bullshit. Another reason is the greater volume of commercial speech on behalf of companies seeking a global market share. Not all commercial speech is bullshit, but a lot of bullshit is commercial speech.

When did you last see an actor say his latest movie was lousy? Now, when did you last see a lousy movie? Suffice it to say the latter happens far more frequently than the former. Commercial speech insists that everything it speaks of is good, and when everything is good, nothing is good. There is also escalating hyperbole going on here, insofar as everything not only has to be good, but better than all the other billions of good things, which leads to a feedback loop of shills for an infinity of proliferating, ever-improved products. I'll see your Diet Coke with Lemon and raise you a Pepsi Twist. I'll see your Pepsi Twist and raise you a Vanilla Coke. And so on, until no corner goes cola-less, and there's a worldwide vanilla shortage.

Another property of commercial speech that leads to bullshit production is that it is not written by the people who have to say or assume responsibility for it. This is also a big problem with most political speech. I am not insisting that everyone draft his own material, though the English teacher in me reckons that anyone who cannot string together a sentence probably shouldn't lead a company or a country. But the number of people working from a script today encourages one to view every public statement as acting, an entire culture emoting like a dinner theater troupe. Hey, everyone—let's put on a show! This division of rhetorical labor means that the brains who think up the words don't have to say them, and the speakers who give voice to the words don't have to think them. All the better to disconnect them from reality, my dear.

Better communications technology and the increased volume of commercial speech are two of the major material causes of bullshit's growth, insofar as they have provided the means of distribution and the capital to produce and distribute more manure. Both these trends picked up speed during the period of postwar prosperity in North America, otherwise known as the long boom. The long boom stretched from the mid-forties to the mid-seventies. One of the reasons why Americans enjoyed such a long boom is that they never really demobbed. It took a great deal of propaganda to convince Americans to enter both World Wars, and a massive mobilization of the forces of production to sustain their participation in these wars. Once the wars were won, the forces of wartime production and persuasion were successfully redeployed in the service of domestic affluence, convenience, and progress. This is not to say that there were no wars, for copious dollars continued to flow into the military-industrial complex, but on the domestic front, peace and prosperity prevailed. Propagandists became PR men and advertisers and we cranked out the cars, televisions, and trinkets of the new consumer culture.

This period laid the infrastructure for the bullshit explosion, but it took a few more unfortunate events, like the fiscal crumminess and stagflation of the late seventies, to finally blow it up real good. The one-two punch of Vietnam and Watergate left public trust in democratic institutions in tatters. The leaders of the eighties, folks like Reagan, Thatcher, and Mulroney, urged us to put our trust in markets instead. Reagan went so far as to claim that government itself was the problem, and markets the solution: "It's time to get government off the backs of the people," quoth the Gipper. The free market was presented as democracy in action, the public sphere vilified as inefficient, cumbersome, retrograde. In fact, the very idea of a public good was dismissed as some hippy-dippy liberal chimera. As Iron Maggie once decreed, there is no such thing as society, only individuals. This sort of individualistic, up-with-markets rhetoric has been the most consistent theme in politics for the past twenty years. Even alleged Democrats like Clinton cut the welfare rolls.

This kind of thinking has significant social side effects, ways of thinking that aid and abet bullshit production. First, saying "let the market decide" is kind of like saying "let the car drive." It's mystical, and it also implies that we should not blame whoever happens to be behind the wheel. Second, it has made us more self-interested, a natural consequence of being told twenty million times that individuals achieve amazing things and generate fabulous wealth, while collective endeavors or shared goals lead to committees, teamsters, and gulags. This is also a result of being informed that you will never be a beneficiary of all the Great Society safety-net fun, like cheap tuition, or free health care, or a pension. You know that it's all up to you, and that you have to believe in you, to quote two of our most beloved inspirational truisms. You have to sell you, since nobody else will, and there is nobody to blame but you if you fail your way into poverty.

This emphasis on the self is by no means confined to politics and economics. Pop culture, from celebrity coverage to the memoir deluge, showcases individuals overcoming the customary impediments, like abuse and addiction and divorce and disease. The language of news broadcasts has shifted selfward, switching from the traditional collective pronouns of hard news to a more personal you-speak and increased coverage of the personal peccadillos of public figures. Pop psychology, otherwise known as self-help, is a publishing and daytime TV juggernaut worth billions. When you do an Amazon search for books about the self, the server spits out more than thirty thousand titles. For those who'd rather spruce up their outsides than their insides, there is the cavalcade of lifestyle porn: Think Martha, pre-slammer, and all the experts that have done Martha.

There is nothing inherently wrong with self-interest. The danger lies in the ego growing outsized, overfed on a steady diet of nothing. It is little wonder that we can be such selfish, shortsighted beings, considering the extent to which we are encouraged to think no further than our image, our comfort, our next snack. We are forever being wooed by new needs, and bombarded by freshly minted wants. This happy consumer plenitude goes beautifully with all the scary political straight talk about supporting yourself or eating dog food in a cardboard box. Self-reliance is the stick, and self-indulgence is the carrot, but the focus remains the same: Does this work for me? What's in it for me? Enough about me—what do I think of me?

Conservative virtuecrats blame today's chronic truth decay on relativism in its many pernicious forms. Some of them castigate the "if it feels good, do it" permissiveness of hippies and boomers. Others point a finger at the godlessness of modern life. Others point to academia, which erroneously assumes that liberal arts faculties have any sway over the culture. If we did, believe me, I would be the first to do a merry power-mad jig in the town square. Alas, we do not.

If we have become a more relativist culture, less inclined to believe in absolutes like God and truth, more inclined to subjective judgments, it is largely due to the millions of choices presented by the market. One of the main articles of postmodern criticism is that there is no capital-T truth, merely competing truth claims. This is the kind of talk that makes conservatives accuse po-mo thought of being politically correct gobbledygook. But this formula does describe their beloved free market very nicely, as every product or service makes a competing claim of sorts, and no one, ideal, holy, true soda prevails. All sales pitches may strain to reach the absolute, à la Coke Is It, but they only have value in relation to one another. Or, to paraphrase philosopher Gilles Deleuze, we have shifted from moral existence to aesthetic existence, where questions of taste engage us more frequently than questions about the good. Ironically, many of the people who, through their policies and their ideologies, have pushed us into this world of constant consumption castigate the decadence that invariably accompanies the very affluence they seek as the greatest of all goods.

This is not to claim that the old dogmas do not persist. This is merely to note that in most North American cities the Christian store, with its Left Behind books and saint decor and Jesus fish for the car, is never more than a drive away from the place that sells the Che T-shirts, face jewelry, and bongs. The free market is powerful and lucrative and fun precisely because it is the great Relativizer, leveler of all values, equally glad to crank out the trappings of kink or conformity, ready to cater to the lewd or the prude. Money does not care whether you are using it to buy a gross of Bibles or of nipple clamps.

One of the great paradoxes of modern life is that money is our major good, since money is equally glad to pal around with the honest dealer and the flimflam artist. Money is me-minded, as well. There's nothing money loves more than hanging around with other money. Money can't get enough of money. It's like a Zen koan: It takes it to make it.

The free market has provided unparalleled levels of affluence, comfort, and peace for North Americans. I am enjoying the blandishments of glorious capitalism even as I type this sentence. Mmmm, comfy couch, big-screen TV, effervescent beverages, mmmm. But, and it is a great big but, it would be a mistake to consider the current setup of the global economy a meritocracy, democracy in action, or a final moral arbiter. The free market ain't that free. You have to pay to get in. The global economy is a crazy patchwork quilt of mixed economies. Every major North American industry is propped up by public infrastructure, like government subsidies, tax entitlements, and protectionist trade regulations. Many North American industries are dominated by a few huge colluding concerns,

which hardly squares with classical economic visions of independence, competition, efficiency, and transparency. Some
North American concerns have entirely abandoned old-
school notions like providing services or products people are
willing to pay for, and instead make their profits via book
cooking, numbers juggling, speculation, liquidation, outsourcing, and downsizing. The latter practices are not just the
mark of corrupt concerns like Enron, WorldCom, or Global
Crossing; most leading CEOs have presided over layoffs in the
thousands, and General Electric has divested itself of almost
half of its workers over the past decade.

Moreover, it is what the free market sets people to doing
that really matters. The last long boom was the result of a vibrant manufacturing sector. The gilded notion of mid-
century family values has everything to do with the fact that
Mom could stay home with the kids and Jesus, baking pies, because Dad made enough dough to provide for the whole brood.
One of the great Republican conundrums is that their aggressively pro-rich economic policies have made it virtually impossible for anyone to live in the kind of good old-fashioned family
that their social policies strive to create. The great Democratic
conundrum is that they have become New High-Fashion Republicans for Girls.

Now more of us work, we spend more time at work, and
more of us work in the service sector, the fastest-growing in
North America. The service sector is not as well paid, has a
lower economic multiplier effect, and involves tons of phony
cheer. The growth of the service sector is certainly implicated
in the production of bullshit, insofar as customer service involves repeating lickspittle mantras. And since you are what
you soak in, a long, hard day of making things is bound to produce a different sort of person than a long, hard day of greeting

folks in the foyer of the Wal-Mart, asking if they want fries with their burger, or conducting phone surveys.

There are several other reasons why there is so much bullshit, not the least of which is that we continue to tolerate it. We might grumble about bullshit, but few of us are inclined to ask for the manager or boycott the offender. This is partly due to a sense that resistance is futile. You, as a lone consumer, can hardly put a dent in any of the reigning oligopolies with your singular refusal, no matter how cruddy their service or product may be. You, as a single voter, can hardly influence matters of state to the same degree that industry concerns and special interest lobbies can. These feelings of impotence, insignificance, and isolation represent the bummer underside of all that self-interest speak, for you are but a superfluous drop in the mighty churning sea that will wash on with or without you. It's the triple-A of apathy, alienation, and atomization.

The business of ordinary life involves speaking to loads of different people we do not know and who do not know us. I realize this is a Well, Duh proposition, but it is an important part of why we continue to produce and perpetuate bullshit. Relative anonymity, or lack of direct contact, lowers the truth stakes. Lying guides emphasize that it is always easier to slide a fib past someone you do not know; someone who knows you well is more likely to notice your tells. More important, you probably wouldn't want to abuse their trust to begin with. We may be connected to many more people, but not enough to develop a sense of trust. It is far easier to fib on the phone than it is in person. It is far easier to fib on the TV or the Web than on the phone.

It is a banal example of a larger phenomenon, but when you hear the familiar words, "your call is important to us," are you, personally, being lied to? Yes and no. The nice people who put you on hold are not out to deceive you. They are merely doing their jobs, which they more likely than not dislike, and with good reason. Employees at call centers are trained to develop a phoniness that is deeply demeaning, for workers and customers both. They have to act like you are King or Queen Customer, because their company has doubtless adopted some Service Quality Excellence Formula, even though your call is but one of the thousands that the cubicle farm will field today. Even when you get past the recording, many phone jockeys aren't really talking to you at all. They, like so many little Gwyneth Paltrows, are simply giving voice to a script, a protocol of politesse expressly designed to defuse a screwed consumer's outrage without actually solving anything.

You, the indignant consumer, probably picked up the phone because this company has your lovely money and you have nothing to show for it. No tickets, no credit card, no dial tone, no reservation, no service, no power, none of the things they promised you in the pretty ads. And hey, what are you going to do, now that you've been waiting on hold this long, chump? Hang up? Get bumped down the priority-sequence queue?

It disproves itself every time it plays, and still, everyone keeps on playing it.

If my call is so important to you, why isn't anyone answering the damn phone?

CHAPTER TWO

PAINTING THE LAWN GREEN

Public Relations and Advertising

*By the way, if anyone here is in marketing or advertising . . .
kill yourself.*

—BILL HICKS

Though we all hold some responsibility for the high bull-shit content of modern life, there are a few vanguard industries that have made exceptional contributions to the piling merde. The most obvious offender is the conjoined-twin leviathan of public relations and advertising, billion-dollar industries that create nary a thing but buzz, hype, images, spin, brands, press releases, campaigns, events, and apologies. Unlike, say, auto manufacturing or chip making or gold mining, PR and advertising are meta-industries—middlemen running interference between the public and corporations, institutions, or individuals. Ads tell us what to buy and who to be. PR tells us who to trust and what to believe. Ads are the happy carnival face of the business world, which remains largely incomprehensible to the layperson. Public relations is the chorus of reassuring experts, the dulcet voices of reason who speak and write on behalf of the powers that be.

Ads are a much bigger business than PR. Total U.S. ad spending grew alongside the nineties' boom, increasing from an estimated $128 billion in 1991 to $247 billion in 2000, when every product, from soup to hair gel to golf balls, ran some bogus millennium-themed promotional campaign. Ad spending dipped by about 16 billion clams in 2001, doubtless due to the effects of prolonged ad-free September 11 coverage. In 2002, spending inched back up to $237 billion. In 2003, onward and upward, the revenues went, to $245 billion. Projections for 2004 are more and better, hovering around $263 billion. U.S. ad sales represent about half of the global market.

In terms of both revenue and spending, PR remains a much more modest affair. An industry trade group, the Council of Public Relations Firms, estimates that global PR revenues were approximately $5.4 billion in 2002. However, PR revenues have been growing steadily since the mid-nineties, precisely because good PR is so much cheaper and more cost-effective than a big, splashy ad campaign.

Advertising and PR make one thing and one thing only, and that is *shit up*. Making shit up is not to be confused with outright lying, though lying is sometimes involved. Making shit up is more like painting the lawn green when the queen comes to town. The grass may well be green to start with, but it ain't *that* green. Ads present something tangential to the truth—something more interesting or enjoyable or photogenic or sentimental than the truth. For example: Yes, that company makes a car. It exists and it is available. I can indeed purchase that Chevy Tacoma, or that Nissan Xterra. But there is a hitch. In the television ads for the Tacoma, where the car tears over rugged, rocky hills, and the Xterra, where the car zips and zags over sand dunes, there are disclaimers that read, "Professional Stunt Driver. Closed Course. Do Not Attempt." The product is real, but the situation pictured is as phony as a chocolate doubloon.

SUV ads are particularly odious. The notorious gas-guzzlers are invariably shown speeding through the glorious natural world that their emissions threaten. One recent SUV ad shows a young man at the reading of a will. The executor announces that he has received a large parcel of swampland. That's not a family fuck-you from beyond the grave, though—the next scene shows an SUV tooling around the bogs, wheels churning up the muck. Yee-haw! cries the dude, while, off-camera, the surrounding marshland flora and fauna suffer multiple embolisms. The swamp ad is but one in a genre; ads also depict SUVs plowing through the forest, the desert, the mountains, the tundra, and the ocean surf.

In an ad for the SUV to end all SUVs, the gargantuan Hummer H2, some sweet little kids gather for a soapbox derby race. There are shots of a young boy cobbling his entry, a soapbox Hummer, together. The kids line up on top of a hill in their adorable little cars. The race begins, and all the kids' cars trundle along the track to the jangling chords of The Who's "Happy Jack," but the rugged young individualist in the homemade Hummer can't be confined by the pedestrian rules of the road. The kid in the Hummer barrels straight down the hill, finishing ahead of all the chumps who stuck to the prescribed course. The charming, twee look of the ad appears to be cribbed from the wonderful movie *Rushmore*, but the message—that one should barrel past others in a tank—is pure hubristic Hummer.

Allow me to share with you a highly unscientific survey of the advertising I have seen during my prime-time sessions of random channel flipping: Apparently, Burger King has a new chicken baguette sandwich that gets its flavor from fire-grilling, not fat. The low-fat angle is part of a more widespread fast-food makeover, but this is not the first time that Burger King, perpetrator of the Croissan'wich, has tried to peddle their grease by pretending it's European. Hair products and cars also claim continental styling, whatever that means. Suffice it to say that the sandwich itself looks about as Parisian as Des Moines, and, unlike the car ads, there is no disclaimer to warn you that the actual sandwich will contain one half the color and freshness of the advertised sandwich, though I know this to be true from my own dining experience.

Next, the trim silver-haired lady in the Celebrex ad plays golf with gay abandon, insisting that joint pain isn't going to make her play nine holes when she really wants to go for the full eighteen. She's feisty, but the ad is not the rapturous ode to joy that Celebrex ads once were. The manufacturers had their knuckles rapped by regulators for making excessive product claims, so the old ads—the ones with seniors Rollerblading and doing tai chi and a chorus that trilled, "Do what you want to do, go where you want to go"—have been yanked. The Celebrex ad ends like all drug ads end. The voice-over warns of the side effects, lists the contraindications, and then encourages you to ask your doctor.

More car ads, endless car ads, bumper-to-bumper pitches for cars, cars, cars. One for the Mitsubishi Endeavor starts with the sleek black behemoth streaking out of a tunnel, under an overpass, toward the open road. Guitars yowl. Then the camera cuts to the interior of the minivan, to a happy young family, and the music changes, to a snippet of the *SpongeBob SquarePants* theme. Don't worry, aging hipsters—you can breed and rock, at the same time, in the same affordable vehicle. Next, we have soccer uniform–clad girls and freckle-faced towheads in plaid shirts experiencing the full-day relief of prescription Strattera. As the ad cuts from footage of the little ADD-lings behaving at school to shots of them behaving at the dinner table, the voice-over warns of side effects. The disclaimer notes that Strattera has not been tested on children under six. Guess you'll have to find other meds for the baby.

Next we have a spot for the Honda Pilot that features a husband who has been raised by wolves, one in a proud tradition of ads based on the premise that men are dumb. In many ads, men are so boneheaded they cannot even be trusted to buy toilet paper on their own. Then McDonald's hops on the hip-hop tip, with their latest rapped ad and their tag line, "I'm lovin' it." A GE ad compares their new smart washer-dryers to a marriage between a computer geek and a supermodel, and then flashes the many insignias of their umpteen diversified brands. Meet Blue Cash, says American Express, to funky pizzicato flutes. Wendy's "unofficial spokesman" stalks snackers, supposedly of his own free will. And then, lip-licking, liquor-pitching sirens appear, misty and writhing with, um, thirst.

The late, great comedian Bill Hicks said that ads were porn, according to the Supreme Court definition: sexual content with no redeeming artistic merit. When he saw the Doublemint twins, he certainly wasn't thinking of gum. This brings me to the Coors twins. For those of you in the cloisters, this classic ad features a song about all the good things in life, like watching TV and drinking beer, and hot, wet, identical twins in as little fabric as the law allows. The difference between the Doublemint twins and the Coors twins is a difference of degree, not kind.

Even the most lunkheaded Yankee ad has production values and professionalism going for it. Canadian advertising is its own little earnest, mid-priced world of awful. Most Canadian ads have the dingy, amateurish mien of cable access footage.

There are way too many dairy board ads. I think I know about eggs, thanks. McCain's, a humongous Canuck food concern, is responsible for a panoply of terrible, low-budget ads for its various edibles, from fries to cakes to pizzas. In one for frozen juice concentrate, a dreadlocked guy plays a merry tune on drinking glasses while a hippie chick saws on a neon-green violin. It ranks among the most uncool attempts to be cool I have ever seen.

Advertising desperately wants to be and purvey cool, and often does so by serenading us with our own music collections. This also smuggles junk into our brains in a Trojan horse of sweet melody. Molson, of all the hockey haircut beers, used the Smiths' mope-pop classic, "How Soon Is Now?" to push their frat-boy suds, even though Molson guzzlers tended to shove pasty Brit-pop fans into lockers. Companies like The Gap, Volkswagen, and Apple plundered the playlists of indie rock snobs in search of catchy tunes, and nothing was too obscure or political to push product. When my activist pals and I were editing footage of lefty protests in the ancient early nineties, the soundtrack question was not which band we should use, but which Clash song. Now "London Calling" is the call of the Jaguar X-Type. Scottish rock darlings Mogwai are featured in a Levi's ad. Nissan is moving minivans with a few bars from Modest Mouse. Some artists have even learned how to game the promo system. The ubiquitous Moby made the transition from obscure vegan electronica guy to U.S. magazine celebrity by selling every single song from his 1999 album, *Play*, to advertisers. This is a deal with the devil, though. Once it is plundered by advertisers, a song will be bound forever to beer or shampoo, or, in Moby's case, countless movie trailers and TV shows, American Express, and a couple of different, competing cars.

Advertisers' zeal to use song titles as slogans sometimes leads to shotgun weddings. It was all well and good to use Iggy Pop's "Lust for Life" in the movie *Trainspotting*, since we were still in the realm of junkiedom, but its use as an anthem for family cruise lines is a thing passing strange. Sure, it's an upbeat number, but your average Carnival cruiser would call 911 if they beheld the writhing specter of Iggy circa 1977. Another famous failed example of this is the Reagan team's request to use "Born in the U.S.A." as their official campaign song, a request the Boss justly denied.

Try though I may, I cannot think of one television ad, of the hundreds of thousands I have seen in a lifetime of couch potato sessions, that I would really like to see again. I am also enervated by the fact that ads are always louder than programming, and that ads tend to run simultaneously on the major networks, so as to discourage fleeing channel flippers. Advertisers have let out a mighty hue and cry over the popularity of digital video recorders, like TiVo, which allow viewers to skip over their masterpieces entirely. In fact, even though ad skipping is one of the main reasons why TiVo devotees love their TiVos, the company recently agreed to run pop-ups to help make up for all the fast-forwarding.

My objection to advertising is not merely aesthetic. Each and every shill is a tax-deductible cost of doing business, and thus a double insult. The billions that companies spend to convince you that you are a smelly, yellow-toothed porker translate into millions fewer for the public purse and drive up the price of products. A pair of Nikes only costs a few bucks to make, but it costs a lot to get Michael Jordan to invest those shoes with the holy Nike aura.

My mystical language is purposeful: Advertising attempts above all to sanctify mass-produced crap with a halo of

uniqueness and beauty, or deliciousness and comfort, or cool-
ness and Xtremity. Ads determine not only what we buy but
how we perceive ourselves and even what we do. There is, for
example, mounting evidence that we may be making ourselves
ill with our ad-induced scrubbing. While we scour the world
to a sterile gleam and mock the mammal scents of our continental friends, research tells us that kids in slightly grimy
houses have a lower incidence of asthma than those who live
in immaculate surroundings. And antibiotic hand washes only
accelerate the development of more resistant bugs, a process
already well under way thanks to the mass prescribing of antibiotics.

When you pay the piper, you call the tune—which means
that ads also determine the content we consume. Thus, Bill
Hicks never got to do his last set on *Late Night with David Letterman,* although he had previously appeared on the show
eleven times. He performed his monologue for Dave and the
audience before the taping began. But at the last minute, his
performance was unceremoniously dumped. Hicks had a bit
about pro-lifers, and one of the show's sponsors was a pro-life
organization. Hicks was so incensed that he wrote a letter
about the perils of truth-telling in the "United States of Advertising" to *The New Yorker* writer John Lahr. "Look at 90 percent
of what's on TV," Hicks wrote. "Banal, puerile, trite scat." Letterman, a big fan, was contrite about the way the producers
handled the situation, but Hicks died of pancreatic cancer, at
the age of thirty-two, before the show could book him again.

Sponsors are not often so flagrantly censorious, as ads usually influence content further upstream. Networks generally
feel compelled to pitch all programs to the lowest common
denominator, or to the most desirable demographic, the
eighteen-to-thirty-four set, so as to satisfy advertisers. To see

the way that network advertiser dollars produce programming pabulum, watch an episode of *Six Feet Under* or *The Sopranos*, made by the commercial-free HBO and compare it to your standard-issue schlubby-guy-married-to-a-beautiful-lady sitcom, or one of the countless cop dramas that are copies of copies of *Law and Order*, or any of the cheap and venal reality shows.

In the same way that most of us consider ourselves excellent bullshit detectors, we generally think ourselves immune to ads. Some shrewd marketing pros have caught on to this resistance, or resentment, and insist that PR is the new brand-building force. Ads are obvious and ubiquitous, but PR cloaks itself in credibility. PR is the stealth form of advertising—a far more subtle art. Its stock in trade is the semi-science and pseudo-research that so often end up in the news. One nice example of this sort of press-release-friendly research is the Credibility Index, produced by a consortium of top PR firms. This is a ranking of occupations according to trustworthiness. Supreme Court justices, teachers, ordinary citizens, and military officials get high trust ratings, according to the survey. Public relations specialists, like the nice people who conducted the research, rank third from the bottom, just ahead of Hollywood phonies like entertainers and talk-show hosts, and well behind other alleged fibbers, like politicians and CEOs.

PR specialists are nothing if not diligent in their attempts to work their way up the Index. This may explain why they bandy about the word *ethics* so freely. On one of the countless websites that do PR for PR, a slogan reads, "Ethical PR: Not an Oxymoron!" When you have to say that sort of thing with an exclamation mark, perhaps your image-making business has an image problem. Both the American and Canadian public relations guilds stress the importance of ethics for the public relations practitioner. The first line of the Public Relations Society of America Members' Code of Ethics Pledge reads, "I pledge to conduct myself professionally, with truth, accuracy, fairness, and responsibility to the public." The predominant model of conduct in most current PR-school literature is journalism. PR counselors, like reporters, must disseminate factually accurate information in a clear and compelling manner. The big difference is that journalists don't engineer the events that they report on. Sure, journalists and their editors choose to cover the corrupt company or the dog show, but they generally don't fabricate stories from whole cloth, Jayson Blair and Stephen Glass notwithstanding. PR is unabashedly a full-service operation: They produce the event and report on it.

It takes PR to turn the mere fact of a new product or a new policy into a bona fide event. And it takes PR to hand the first drafts of reportage to the media. PR is like having your very own personal reporter, writing *The You Times*, where the news, even if it's bad, even if it's not news at all, still makes you look good. And if you're a big PR firm like Burson-Marsteller, then you are writing *The You Times* for folks like Romanian dictator Nicolae Ceaușescu, those responsible for the Bhopal disaster, the Saudi royal family, the people who produce bovine growth hormones, and Exxon after the *Valdez* spill.

There have, of course, been spokespeople and promoters since the dawn of time. The word *propaganda* comes from the efforts of the Catholic Church, under Pope Gregory XV, to propagate the faith in the wake of the Reformation. Publicity materials and handbills were used by manufacturers of soap and patent medicines in North America throughout the eighteenth and nineteenth centuries. But public relations and advertising as established, lucrative professions grew huge over the last century, expanding alongside media technologies like radio, television, and the Internet. Advertising got a head start: The first ad agency in the United States opened in Philadelphia in 1841. By the 1890s, J. Walter Thompson, the oldest North American ad agency still operating, was billing a million dollars a year. By the turn of the century, Coca-Cola's advertising budget was up to 100,000 dollars a year, and newcomer Pepsi hit the market in 1902, starting the glorious century-long advertising bonanza that is the Cola War.

The Publicity Bureau, the first PR firm in North America, also opened at the turn of the century, in 1901. The Boston office practiced a sort of proto-PR, helping clients look good in the muckraking dailies of the time. It's difficult to determine the parentage of an entire profession, and this goes double for a field like public relations, since a couple of early PR men laid claim to the title "Father of PR" when doing their own PR. The two most serious contenders, though, in terms of sheer influence and longevity, are "Poison" Ivy Lee and Edward L. Bernays.

Lee was a reporter who got into the nascent publicity biz in 1903. He counted Bethlehem Steel, the Pennsylvania Railroad, and American Tobacco among his clients. He also implemented the Rockefeller family makeover in 1914; after thirteen women and children were killed in a labor protest at a Rockefeller mine in Ludlow, Missouri, and the robber barons took a beating in the press and public opinion, Ivy did damage control and rehabilitated their public image. After first spinning the massacre into a blow for "industrial freedom," Lee's strategy was simple: Actions speak louder than words. The Rockefellers' subsequent actions—oodles of cash for philanthropic initiatives, the pursuit of political office—have made the Ludlow mine disaster the obscurest of labor history footnotes, and the name Rockefeller synonymous with dynastic East Coast wealth. The rich guy on *The Flintstones* was a Rockefeller; Jay-Z, one of the most successful East Coast rappers, probably didn't dub his posse the Roc-A-Fella crew to invoke strike-breaking incidents of yore.

Bernays didn't open his New York office until 1919, but he was a far more diligent archivist, and a more enthusiastic booster for PR, than Lee. Bernays wrote extensively on the subject of PR and taught the first university course in PR, at New York University, in 1923. Bernays, of all the early PR men, was most committed to doing PR for PR. Moreover, Bernays outlived all his contemporaries, dying in 1995 at the ripe age of 103. He continued to lecture, give interviews, and open up his archives to PR students until his death, and witnessed the transformation of PR into the multibillion-dollar business it is today.

Bernays started out doing flak for the ballet, even though he hated dance, and then went to work for the U.S. Committee for Public Information, the government's press agency during the war effort. When World War I ended, Bernays began working for American Tobacco, the makers of Lucky Strikes. Bernays's job was to capitalize on the wartime uptick in cigarette sales and try to get the ladies, a hitherto untapped market, smoking. Bernays came up with the campaign "Reach for a Lucky Instead of a Sweet," and staged a media nonevent; several beautifully dressed young ladies lit cigarettes on Fifth Avenue while promenading on an Easter Sunday afternoon—a real no-no in 1929, even though more women were smoking indoors—to express their glorious freedom from the dictates of the patriarchy. Coffin nails, schmoffin nails; those butts were "torches of freedom." Cigarette sales surged. Luckies were the number one brand in 1930.

Decades later Bernays's strategy remains the gold standard when it comes to selling cigarettes to women. The appetite-suppressing charms of the cigarette are demonstrated by the only remaining public female smokers, super-skinny actresses and models who maintain their IKEA-sparse frames with a steady diet of champagne, water, and Marlboros. Cigarette manufacturers still use feministy slogans to shill smokes to the fairer sex, the best example of this being the seemingly inter- minable "You've Come a Long Way, Baby" campaign by Vir- ginia Slims. Smoking, in spite of the fact that it is an addiction, continues to be marketed in the argot of freedom and rebel- lion, nonconformity and escape, popularized by Edward L. Bernays in the 1930s.

Interestingly, while flogging cigarettes, Bernays insisted that his own wife quit smoking. He was worried about her health. Conscience and professionalism finally coincided when, in 1964, Bernays masterminded anti-tobacco campaigns that at- tempted to inform people of the deleterious effects of smoking.

Bernays worked for more than four hundred clients during his forty years of full-time practice, among them General Mo- tors, NBC, CBS, General Electric, Proctor & Gamble, and *Time* and *Cosmopolitan* magazines. Tactics that remain corner- stones of PR, like targeted direct mailing, product placement, and public opinion polling, were pioneered by Bernays. Ac- cording to Bernays, PR wasn't just a question of representing corporate interests to the public; he insisted that corporations had to read up on public hopes, desires, and impressions, and use this information to come up with the most powerful rhet- oric and effective symbols to sway that public. A good PR man was as much a social scientist as he was an impresario. Bernays, who was Sigmund Freud's nephew, was particularly interested in the psychology of the crowd. He worked to popu- larize his uncle's psychoanalytic theories in the United States and, at the same time, adopted some of the ur-shrink's ideas in crafting the art and science of spin. In 1932, John Flynn, a writer for *The Atlantic Monthly,* wrote that Bernays worked to unearth the subconscious desires of the masses, just as his uncle had investigated individual subconscious desires through psychoanalysis.

For Bernays, spin wasn't just a business but a valuable public service. In books like *Propaganda, Crystallizing Public Opinion,* and *The Engineering of Consent,* Bernays argued that PR men helped maintain social order by anticipating the desires of the herd and voicing them to the corporate powers-that-be. PR men were the intelligent, select few, the interpreters who could forge the inchoate masses into a single mind. While Bernays insisted that the thoughtful public relations counselor should turn down suspicious clients—he refused gigs for Franco and Nixon—and stated that the goal of PR was to inform the public, not fool it, his definition of propaganda suggests otherwise. He wrote, "The only difference between 'propaganda' and 'education,' really, is in the point of view. The advocacy of what we believe in is education. The advocacy of what we don't believe in is propaganda." Bernays wasn't employing propaganda in its popular, pejorative sense. He wrote this passage in the twenties, and propaganda would not become a dirty word until after World War II, when the term became inextricably linked with Fascist movements in Europe. Propaganda was simply what PR men made for a living. Despite Bernays's oft-repeated injunctions against swindling the public, or telling lies in the service of a client, his definition of propaganda underlines the fact that PR men enthused for a living. The PR man's job was not to believe but to make beliefs, to document and sway the beliefs of the masses, and to craft believable, sympathetic public profiles for corporate or political entities. It was a far more sweeping endeavor than advertising.

With the growth of broadcast media over the last century, and the increase in available paid space, advertising became the more lucrative and visible of the two professions, though they remain intimately intertwined. Many PR consultants work under the umbrella of ad firms, and PR strategies sometimes involve advertising. Unlike ad firms, PR firms generally fly under the radar. Clinton's cadre of consultants, among them James Carville, still get screen time, thanks to all the coverage their coverage-making got. But the vast majority of PR simply bleeds into the news. Good PR, like expertly applied makeup, doesn't look like PR at all.

Let's take a spin through a PR campaign waged by ConAgra, the second largest food company in North America, which in 2001 was named winner of both *PR Week's* 2001 Campaign of the Year and the PRSA's coveted Silver Anvil Award. (Why the Silver Anvil, you ask? Well, that's because PR experts *forge* public opinion, shaping it into useful things like horseshoes or snaffle bits or market shares.) To secure these awards, the nice people at ConAgra, who make brands like Butterball and Healthy Choice, teamed up with a PR firm called Cone to produce a real lollapalooza: "ConAgra's Feeding Children Better." The great idea that fueled this program—what Bernays would have called its "Big Think"—was that 12 million kids in the U.S. still went to bed hungry every night, despite the nineties' boom. ConAgra had thrown some leftover turkeys at the cause before, but these scattershot efforts, noble though they may have been, weren't sufficient. The PR people at Cone led ConAgra through an intensive research, planning, and program development process they called Cause Maximization™. ConAgra decided to donate to hunger relief efforts, buying trucks for organizations like Second Harvest, and began promoting the now-Maximized Cause™ of child hunger, thus linking its name, and its brands, to the alleviation of said scourge. But before they could begin ladling out free soup for the wee ones, Cone and ConAgra had to make sure that their targeted, strategic approach was proprietary and ownable. Fortunately, it had not occurred to Christ to patent the feeding-the-hungry thing and all was smooth legal sailing. Then, using child hunger as a rallying point for their internal corporate culture, and as a sympathetic spin on their many brands, ConAgra proceeded to rack up more than 85 million media impressions for Feeding Children Better.

ConAgra did donate more than 200 tons of food to the launch of Feeding Children Better, and was consequently named Donor of the Year by Second Harvest. All this is swell and good, but ConAgra, despite their acts of munificence, remains a giant corporation in the business of business, doing good for the express purpose of those 85 million media impressions. This maneuver, a philanthropic gesture to bolster the company's good name and lend an aura of social responsibility to the concern that sells you your transfats and your high-fructose corn syrup, is classic PR. Whenever you hear anything about a company doing something nice from the goodness of its heart, you are seeing the fruits of weeks of meetings to determine how best the company can make nice. ConAgra's charitable works were, in PR parlance, a natural fit. Hungry kids + kind megafood corp = publicity gold.

Cause Maximization™ wouldn't have impressed Immanuel Kant much; a moral action is not properly moral if the actor is showing off in the interest of being seen as moral.

Funny thing: At the same time that this glorious initiative against Child Hunger was being launched, the Centers for Disease Control released some pretty compelling statistics about child obesity. Fourteen percent of American children were morbidly obese, with all the attendant health hazards the condition implies. There were more big fat kids than there were little hungry ones, but child obesity would hardly have been a natural fit for ConAgra. After all, ConAgra made Orville Redenbacher popcorn and distributed the vast majority of french fries available at fast-food outlets; how would a "Feeding Children Less" campaign have played, given that most obese kids were wearing a couple of pounds of ConAgra fries?

Of course, PR is not all free hot lunch for the urchins. PR is also responsible for engineering nonevents like the Millennium Dreamers Campaign, which brought together McDonald's, Walt Disney, and UNESCO. This league of giants united to, um, recognize children. Seriously. Outstanding kids from all over the world were nominated to be part of a delegation of two thousand. Phase two saw the names of the two thousand children revealed at a special event at the United Nations New York headquarters. This was notable, claimed the campaign summary, since the event marked the first joint public appearance of corporate icons Ronald McDonald and Mickey Mouse. The final phase of the Millennium Dreaming was a youth summit at Walt Disney World Resort in Florida, where the children received medals for outstanding contributions to their communities and took part in a symposium on leadership in the glorious future.

What kind of outstanding contributions did these youngsters make? Millennium Dreamers are those nice kids you always see in the newspaper, raising funds for the sick and the poor, campaigning against violence and war, working for worthy causes. It's nice of the Rat and the Clown to spring for a party in honor of these most excellent moppets, but it doesn't really change the fact that they are pimping out the sweetest kids in the world to maintain their iron grip on the fantasy lives and temper tantrums of kids all over the globe. And despite more than 2 billion media impressions, damned if I can remember even one of those talented kids. I do remember Mickey and Ronald, though, and, as the summary notes, "The objectives behind the program included increasing awareness of McDonald's and Disney on the part of kids and families around the world; enhancing the value of the McDonald's/Disney partnership both internally and externally; and capturing media attention."

Think, for a minute, of your good friend, your brain. Picture it as real estate. Who's installed in the waterfront property, synaptically speaking? I'd wager that if you sat down and tried to write a list of three McDonald's slogans or commercials from memory, it would not take you very long. Previous generations could recite poems and epics from memory; in my twilight years, when I am senile and misrecognizing my own family members, I will doubtless still be able to recall "You Deserve a Break Today." Now try to remember three UN slogans or campaigns. Do they arrive with the same brisk dispatch? If so, you are a better citizen than I am, and I salute you.

Ad creep continues apace, into every nook and cranny of public life. There are ads on washroom doors, billboards ferried by tractor-trailers, and cars wrapped in signage. There are ads on park benches, ads that encase entire buses, and product placement endorsements in the content between the ads. Moreover, ads, like eighties' pop songs and celebrity gossip and comedic catchphrases, are quicker and stickier and flashier than anything else we see. What chance does slow, plodding knowledge have against "Wasssup?" or "I'd Like to Teach the World to Sing?" or "Zoom Zoom Zoom"? Like armies of mnemonic ninjas, they drop out of nowhere and into your head before you even know what hit you.

Some ads, by virtue of the products they shill, remain teth-ered to quotidian reality. It's hard to jazz up an adult diaper; all one can really do is find a nice-looking white-haired lady, have her deliver a few euphemistic phrases about freedom and con-trol, and cut to some shots of spry, vibrant seniors. It is when the product is completely beyond the bounds of need that ad-vertising truly excels, soaring to heights of Wagnerian spec-tacle. Check out the Cola War; nobody needs Pepsi or Coke, but everyone wants 'em, even though, as comic strip *Bloom County* once had it, "both taste like malted battery acid." The 2001 Oscar night Pepsi ad, a Britney Spears production, fea-tures people watching a Britney Spears Pepsi ad. A cook stands slack-jawed, gawking, while his burgers burn. A soccer mom sings along—girl power! Bob Dole, a former spokesperson for Viagra, leers at the little nymphet and says, "Easy, boy" to his randy dog, while she shakes her sequined moneymaker and chirps about the Joy of Cola. The music, the dancing, the light-ing, the huge celebratory hullabaloo over absolutely nothing; pure Cola, millions of dollars visibly and gleefully spent to produce a sixty-second ditty about cheap brown sugar water. Pepsi's not just willing to burn money; they set Michael Jack-son on fire to get our attention.

In the interest of being fairish, I give ads points for being blatant. This thunk-you-on-the-head obviousness isn't a virtue, but it seems like a lesser evil when compared to PR, which bears a great responsibility for reducing the past decade's political discourse to a pageant of fraudulence and play-acting. If a politician receives the press without a spokesman or handler of some sort, it is only because his han-dlers have told him it would look better to greet the public sans entourage—so it's time for an equally phony round of pancake-flipping and har-dee-har-har with the good people on Main St. Is it any wonder that almost half the people in North America can't be arsed to vote? Even Bernays, back in the day, warned that public opinion polling could be dangerously addictive for political machines, resulting in a situation where our leaders no longer lead decisively but merely follow the whims and fancies of the people as expressed in the polls.

Moreover, PR firms have gone beyond the old bag of tricks as their industry has expanded. Hiring "independent" experts, or forming seemingly public-minded committees to shill and front for industry has been part of the way PR works since Bernays got into the business. If a paid spokesperson says it, it's advertising. If experts or committees who have been paid surreptitiously say it, it's PR. There are as many industry front committees are there are industries. A few examples include the Alliance for Better Foods, a consortium of farming, biotech, and grocery concerns, which advocates for more delicious genetic modification. The American Council on Science and Health, a consortium of scientists paid for by chemical and pharmaceutical manufacturers, soothes worries about pills and pesticides. The National Wilderness Institute, a conservative pro-forestry think tank, bills itself as a "voice of reason on the environment." This is a trope common to all such groups, be they pro-drug, pro-pollution, pro-biotech, or antiregulation. Critics of corporations are accused of presenting junk science, hysterical scares, and trivial concerns. Front groups respond with sound science, solid research, and the assurance that all is well.

Medialink, one of the world's most successful PR agencies, has improved on the press release from the front committee with a little number called the VNR, or video news release. These are pretaped segments that wrap a product in a problem or a cause or the bombast of ostensible breakthrough. They are distributed to news outlets all over the country, and sneak their way into your evening news. As Medialink's website brags, "Every major television station in the world now uses VNRs regularly, and most are from Medialink. It's a fact." Ironic they should use the f-word, considering that VNRs aren't even infotainment, let alone hard facts. They are info-advertainment with the gall to pretend to be news.

There are also firms that specialize in fabricating grassroots activists to maximize a cause that is actually a corporate interest. What could be more credible than the spontaneous support of concerned citizens? PR firms such as Burson-Marsteller, Davies Communications, and the Bivings Group produce a reasonable focus-grouped facsimile of just that. Such groups include the Coalition for Health Insurance Choices, who helped undermine Clinton's health care proposals on behalf of the Health Insurers' Association of America. Microsoft had a grassroots strategy to diffuse the bad press around their antitrust trial, which was preempted when someone leaked it to *The Los Angeles Times.* More recently, the exact same letter to the editor appeared, supporting the president, in newspapers across America. Clever bloggers tracked the form letter to a Republican website, which allowed to you to click and send copies of the missive to the publications of your choice. Hell, even the White House engages in this sort of thing. Recently, the Office of Drug Control Policy got their knuckles rapped for distributing a VNR of their own on the perils of pot, and conservative pundit Armstrong Williams revealed that he was paid $240,000 to shill No Child Left Behind.

Other front groups, such as Citizens Against Lawsuit Abuse, Citizens for a Sound Economy, and the Center for Consumer Freedom, who work for tort reform and deregulation on behalf of big business, capture, in their very names, this attempt to purchase the veneer of public support. Groups like Citizens for Sensible Energy Choices, and the Greening Earth Society, though they may sound like a bowl of crunchy granola, are funded by the energy industry and organized by PR firms. Truly, they are doing the good work, passing the conch to the just plain folks. How simply swell to know that even the soccer moms, grandmas, children, and concerned citizens who fulminate at municipal council meetings have been tricked out with a set of talking points and the strategic, paid-for message of PR.

By the way, this little trick is called astroturfing. And that's the quickest way to get an absolutely perfect, changeless lawn, to ensure that all is wonderfully green. Dispense with the grass altogether.

CHAPTER THREE

IF YOU'VE GOT THE MONEY, HONEY

A Fond Look at the Boom and Subsequent Bust

Them that's got shall get, them that's not shall lose. . . .
—Billie Holiday

If the perks of the "ownership society" included your very own genie, what would you wish for? I'm no psychic, but I bet most of you are trying to decide between tens and hundreds of millions. Oh, a few noble souls might request world peace, or true love, or brains, or beauty. But most people would cut straight to the cash, and then maybe found their own eponymous World Peace Foundation, or purchase a succession of spouses, staff, and surgery. Why ask your genie for specific things, when you can simply request the Root of All Things? It's why we do things we don't particularly feel like doing with people we don't particularly care for. It's what your grandma gives you for Christmas, since it's the only thing she's sure you're going to like. People all over North America differ wildly in other matters of taste, but everybody seems to like the exact same kind of money: More. Now. Please.

Alas, in March 2001, newspapers began running obituaries for our irrationally exuberant friend, the economic boom. The

American economy, which had been growing steadily for a decade, finally began to shrink. The financial pages were thick with talk of recession. Unemployment went up and interest rates were laid low, in an attempt to stimulate the flagging economy. The stock market eluded the total meltdown some predicted in the wake of September 11, but the Internet bubble's bust and a succession of corporate scandals dragged the market ever downward. The value of the stock market declined for three years in a row after the bust in 2000, making this bear market the longest since those of 1929–32 and 1938–42.

Pundits initially insisted this recession would be short and shallow. The official recession, according to the National Bureau of Economic Research, lasted from March to November of 2001, but the U.S economy remained sluggish and laggard until the second quarter of 2003. The Bush administration claimed this blip of GDP growth as a miraculous recovery, and evidence of the efficacy of its perfidious tax cuts. It is important to note that this so-called recovery remains a jobless one thus far. In fact, some have even dubbed it the job-loss recovery. Between February 2001 and September 2003, Bush presided over the loss of 2.7 million jobs. The number of Americans living in poverty also increased three years running, to almost 36 million. The trade deficit and the federal debt have also ballooned by the billions, surpassing even the Gipper's record-breakers. The debt, as of January 2005, was $7,601,173,485,023.73, and the trade deficit reached a record-breaking $617 billion in 2004. Democrats argued, throughout the 2004 campaign, that Bush's economic record was worse than that of any presidency since Herbert Hoover's.

Nevertheless, the 2003 recovery, tepid though it may have been, came not a minute too soon for Karl Rove and the rest of the Bush reelection team: It was the perfect justification for four more years of Reaganomic fiscal chicanery. Even though Bush inveighed against those who blame others during the 2000 campaign, and called for a new culture of responsibility, he was quick to pin the moribund economy on anything and anyone but his administration. They inherited the recession from Clinton. And there was 9-11, of course. War. War again. Bush made several references to hitting the "trifecta"—a national emergency, a recession, and a war—as a rationale for record deficit spending and subpar economic growth. He also claimed that he warned the public of the disastrous effects of the trifecta during the 2000 campaign, but no researcher has ever been able to substantiate this.

Bush certainly speaks like a populist when it comes to the economy, in keeping with his whole bullshit aura of brush-clearing folksiness. He is forever talking about his tax cuts in terms of giving just plain folks their money back, even though his tax cuts overwhelmingly benefit the wealthy. The first MBA president also delights in dispensing Econ 101 nuggets about how markets work. My favorite example is this exchange with reporters in a rib joint in Roswell in January 2004. After chiding the "high-paid" reporters for not ordering anything, he schools the press pool:

THE PRESIDENT: Stretch, thank you, this is not a press conference. This is my chance to help this lady put some money in her pocket. Let me explain how the economy works. When you spend money to buy food it helps this lady's business. It makes it more likely somebody is going to find work. So instead of asking questions, answer mine: Are you going to buy some food?
Q: Yes.

THE PRESIDENT: Okay, good. What would you like?
Q: Ribs.
THE PRESIDENT: Ribs? Good. Let's order up some ribs.

Yes, the laws of supply and demand are just this simple. If you can get the chintzy liberal media to pony up for some ribs, we are on the road to economic stability. Put some money in the nice lady's pocket, Stretch.

If only Dubya would heed his own advice, and make with some kind of stimulus that actually benefits the rib-joint ladies of the land. He isn't cutting the payroll tax, which bites into every buck the rib-joint lady makes. No, he's slashing taxes like the dividend tax, and the estate tax, which were created for the express purpose of ensuring that the wealthy contribute their fair share to the public purse. The official recession might have ended a long time ago, but more disturbing economic trends continue unabated, and will only be exacerbated by a second Bush term.

Income inequality continues to grow at an alarming pace. The widening of the gap between the rich and the poor began in the eighties, narrowed slightly during the boom, and has only grown worse since the bust. The level of income inequality in the United States today, the distance from the top to the bottom, is comparable to what it was before the Great Depression led to increased regulation of the plutocrats, and the long boom produced the thriving middle class of the fifties and sixties. The U.S. might have the world's biggest, most boisterous GDP, but a goodly chunk of it belongs to the super-rich, as the U.S. is home to the world's highest concentration of billionaires. The boom may have been lauded and praised as a period of wealth generation and increased productivity, but barely any of the booty trickled down to the middle and lower classes that were producing things. Wealth was generated, but it was also concentrated.

In fact, wealth is even more concentrated than income. In 2001, the wealthiest 1 percent of Americans owned 33 percent of the nation's total wealth. The fortunate 4 percent just beneath them held 26 percent of the spoils. The bottom 62 percent, over a hundred million strong, had only 15 percent of the wealth. The majority of the recent economic gains have been made by the super-richest of the rich, the 1 percent of one, the monster-home, island-compound, and Gulfstream-jet set. In short, the boom was a fantastic time to make money if you already had the money, honey.

We shall return to the pressing problem of inequality, and record deficits and debts of varying types, but let us first recall the good times. Forget the bears. Let's go back to the sweet, sweet bull. The nineties were a pleasingly plump decade, and there were even those who claimed that the boom proper was—and would be—longer than that, discounting the relatively shallow eight-month recession in 1990. One delightful piece of bombast from a 1997 issue of *Wired* magazine pretended to document "The Long Boom," which went all the way from 1980 to 2020. "The Long Boom" started with Reagan, then the Internet changed everything, and by the end we were enjoying unprecedented global prosperity and girding our loins to colonize Mars. It all sounded very Tomorrow Land, in keeping with the strain of utopian libertarian capitalism that echoed through the Valley throughout the boom.

As odd as I find it to pitch my tent next to that of the nice folks who post at godblessronaldreagan.com (who insist the boom was all his doing), our prevailing cultural obsession with money and markets is, indeed, about twenty years old.

The first phase of the bull market began in 1982, after the woes of the energy crisis and stagflation finally subsided. The eighties saw the election of some market-friendly conservative politicians, like Reagan and Thatcher and Mulroney, who made it very clear that the postwar period of New Deal–style social spending was over. This policy shift was a cultural shift, too. The U.S. started moving away from the manufacturing economy that had sustained the last long boom. The Rust Belt was so five minutes ago. The economy was all about Wall Street now, the white-collar wing of the growing service and information economy.

At the same time, the establishment of cable news networks resulted in increased financial coverage. Pop culture–wise, the ratings for shows like *Dallas, Dynasty,* and *Lifestyles of the Rich and Famous* made it clear that conspicuous consumption was one of our favorite spectator sports. But if the face of eighties' wealth was the lizardy mug of Gordon Gekko gravely intoning "Greed is good," the icon of the nineties' boom was the frankly nerdy and owlishly unthreatening Bill Gates, asking you where you wanted to go today. Out with the slicked-back hair and power suits of the previous masters of the universe; this was a relaxed-fit boom all the way, where the millionaires looked like your neighbors, men in blue and beige, fellow travelers from the high school AV club. If fabulous wealth could visit the nerds from your eleventh-grade class, then surely it could visit you, too. Throughout the eighties, the public examples of richness were mostly old white guys in suits and their lacquered, bejeweled wives. In the nineties, those same old guys continued to prevail, but the boom gave us different success stories, and another financial capital. The Street still mattered, but it was the Valley that pumped up the boom and spread the idea that anyone could be a millionaire. The myth of Bill

Gates, college dropout, cobbling together code in his garage, is the boom-era version of the classic Horatio Alger story. Except that the college, in this case, was Harvard, after a stint in private school.

Money and business were prevailing cultural obsessions throughout the balmy boom. CEOs, like the ubiquitous Gates, began appearing not just on the covers of financial magazines but in the mainstream press. Money was never far from the movies, be that in the form of box-office grosses, increasing special-effects budgets and star salaries, or cinematic catchphrases like "Show me the money," courtesy of the Oscar-winning *Jerry Maguire,* and "It's money, baby," from the indie hit *Swingers.* There were countless celluloid paeans to the failed heist, each with loving close-ups of cases full of bills and Motown soundtracks full of payback funk. On TV, *Who Wants to Be a Millionaire* was both a big hit and a purely rhetorical question. Rap music dropped the original gangster pose for ghetto fabulousness, an odd blend of stone-cold thug and CEO, best exemplified by moguls like P. Diddy and Jay-Z. Diddy, the Homey of the Hamptons, bling-blinged and big-pimped in as much white mink and diamonds as Carol Channing. Songs like "It's All About the Benjamins," "Money, Cash, Hoes," and "Dead Presidents"—"Dead presidents represent me," raps Jay-Z—made it clear that rap stars, like the rest of their contemporary North American coevals, had their minds on their money and their money on their minds. And right next to the already famous, attractive people singing choruses to the joys of cash, there was a cast—or is that caste?—of characters famous for wealth and wealth alone.

Part of the reason that money was so very money was simply that there was more of it, and closer at hand. With the explosive growth of the ATM, it was more convenient than ever to withdraw funds—which was precisely what most people were doing, as withdrawals accounted for the majority of terminal activity. No longer did you need to wait in the line of shuffling supplicants at the bank, contemplating the wisdom of your withdrawals in the velvet-roped corral under a teller's cool and appraising gaze; the cashbots spread everywhere, ready to spit your spondulicks at you wherever, whenever. Resistance to the cashbots—with their extra charges for adulterous withdrawals from private terminals or other banks—is futile. Banks across North America have slashed tellers and hours, forcing their customers to succumb to person-free automated convenience and pay for the privilege of so doing.

But I digress; the hordes of bank machines were not yet equipped to *print* the cash. The money was coming from somewhere. First, more people joined the workforce, as women went off to work in increasing numbers, and a double-income family became the norm. According to the U.S. Federal Reserve's Survey of Consumer Finances, the number of households with a pretax income above $25,000 increased to 39 percent in 1982, up from less than 5 percent in 1969, even though only 10 percent of households boasted a pretax income over $50,000 per year. By 1998, more than 50 percent of households made at least $25,000 a year, with 25 percent of those families making between 50K and 100K, and 8.6 percent raking in upwards of six digits.

It wasn't just that more people were making more money. It wasn't enough to make money anymore—your money had to go out and make money, too. Throughout the nineties, people looked at their lazy-ass money, snoozing away in their savings accounts, and told that money to get off the couch, quit eating bonbons, and get to work. In 1989, only 30 percent of the households covered by the Fed survey owned mutual funds or stock. By 1998, that number was near 50 percent. In 1989, 30 percent of households making between 25 and 50K had some tie to the market, through stock, mutual funds, or retirement accounts; in 1998, that figure rose to 52.7 percent. Half of those making between 50K and 100K had stocks in 1989; in 1998, that figure rose to 74.3 percent.

There's nothing quite like people rushing out to buy stock to make more people rush out to buy stock. The market was no longer the province of the elite, of fat-cat capitalists like something out of a Sergei Eisenstein movie, gnawing their cheroots and wearing top hats and monocles. No, this new boom was supposedly for everybody, and the mutual fund ads proudly unfurled the regular faces of their just plain share-holders in countless campaigns. The nineties ushered in the concept that one should commence saving for retirement at an age more commonly associated with paying back student loans. If the pierced and tattooed youngsters in the ads didn't start in on their retirement plans pronto, they could look for-ward to dog food for dinner throughout their golden years, since there certainly wouldn't be pensions by then.

The nineties also brought us the socially responsible mutual fund, in its many odd forms. There's the Aquinas fund, for Catholics, and the Noah fund, for Judeo-Christian investors unhampered by all those antiquated precepts about usury. This impulse was truly ecumenical; I also located IslamiQStocks, a Shari'ah-compliant fund (off-limits to U.S. and U.K. investors post–September 11), based in the ancient holy capital of the Cayman Islands. Old-school traders Smith Barney offer the Concert Social Awareness Fund, which raises the pleasing prospect of a Concert Social Awareness Fund Shareholders' Concert, featuring ethical entertainers like Don Henley or Sting. Lest any identity limp along without its appropriate portfolio, there were also a selection of green, cruelty-free, and women's specials.

This is not to castigate the good intentions of those who choose to invest by putting their money where their beliefs are, though it makes for a strange picture. During the boom, even the youngsters and feminists and hippies and greens and liberals and Holy Rollers who had once castigated markets for being, like, boring or patriarchal or oppressive or polluters or beasts of Babylon started playing the markets, too, provided they could afford to so do. Constituencies that used to object to the market on principle became market niches, and valuable ones at that. In February 2000, Vancouver's Ethical Funds Inc. even went so far as to seek an injunction against Mackenzie Finance Corporation for bogarting the all-important *e*-word. Ethical Funds argued that they were the rightful owners of the registered trademarks "ethical" and "ethical funds" with respect to financial services. They'd been up and running under that name since 1986, after all, and had developed a dozen tobacco-free, no-nukes funds with $2.2 billion in assets.

This increase in participation meant that there was more money frolicking in the market than ever before. According to the SEC's delightful primer, "The Facts on Saving and Investing," mutual fund assets alone expanded from $135 billion in 1980 to a staggering $5.6 trillion in 1999. There was way more money in the market than in bank deposits, which stood at $3.7 trillion. More people were interested in spending or investing than they were in doing anything so hopelessly retro as simply saving their money, even though, as "The Facts" repeatedly notes, the vast majority of American investors remained fiscal illiterates. In September 1998, when savings should have been gangbusters on account of everyone doing so well, the personal savings rate was negative for the first time since the

Dirty Thirties. For every 100 bucks an American made, he blew that and another 20 cents to boot.

Which brings us to debt. Three-quarters of American households—only slightly more than a decade earlier—carried debt, but their *level* of indebtedness rose sharply. If you made anything less than a hundred grand a year, you could expect debts to eat up approximately 17 to 19 percent of your pretax household income. According to a 2001 study by the Pew Research Center, 28 percent of Americans said they owed more than they could afford to pay back, up from 21 percent in 1992. Bankruptcies have continued to climb, even though Congress passed far stricter—which is to say, more bank-friendly—legislation in 1997. There are at least a million a year, even under the tough new rules. In fact, 2003 was a record-breaking year for bankruptcies in the U.S., with 1,650,279 filings.

Consider one specific type of debt: margin debt, money people borrow to play the markets. People weren't just trading their kids' school money, or their retirement funds, during the boom; they were also borrowing to trade. In fact, margin debt was the fastest-growing type of debt in the U.S. from 1993 to 2000. Household and credit debt grew about 60 percent, but margin debt grew six times faster than that, increasing by 362 percent. Hovering below $50 billion until the end of the eighties, it had swollen to $283.5 billion by the turn of the millennium. In January 2000, margin debt comprised 1.4 percent of the value of the stock market—worse than the 1.3 percent just before the crash of 1987. In fact, this is comparable to the margin debt rates before the Securities Act of 1934 was written to regulate borrowing to buy stock and discourage the kind of speculative gambling that caused the 1929 crash.

The increases in market participation and the growth of margin debt are examples of a collective turn away from the actual economy of production and consumption, toward the speculation and fluctuations of the market. Capital rushed into, and then out of, an irrationally exuberant casino economy. When the boom went bust, the biggest losses were in the sectors that were the objects of the most fervent hype, like the tech sector and megacapitalized stocks. While new technologies like the Internet have helped to increase productivity and open up new markets, plenty of tech IPOs were eventually revealed to be little more than Ponzi schemes wrapped in PR. People who got in on Microsoft may have been rewarded several dividends over for their tech savvy, but there is only one Microsoft, and Microsoft has done everything in its considerable powers to ensure that there will only ever be one Microsoft. There are many Pet.coms and lesser WorldComs.

Another sign of this turn away from production toward speculation, from the factory to the casino, are the elephantine bonuses awarded to CEOs throughout the boom. The practice of granting stock options in the company was proposed as a way to ensure that the CEO would act in the interests of that company. By becoming a sort of übershareholder, the CEO would better serve the interests of shareholders. This theory addresses Adam Smith's criticism of the joint stock company, that its holders did not have the same level of interest in the company's welfare as a sole proprietor did. But by the end of the boom it was clear that this ostensible bond between the shareholders and the CEO had almost entirely eclipsed the companies themselves and, by extension, the employees who worked for them. CEO pay didn't just get fat; stock options and other bonuses made pay packages morbidly obese. In 1980, CEOs made 42 times the average worker's pay; by 1990, it had doubled; by 2000, their compensation had increased to 531 times the average salary. The nice people at the AFL-CIO have a calculator on their website that allows you to plug in your own meager 1996 wages and give yourself a CEO-style raise. Try it with a piffling $25,000, and you end up with almost six figures. Now try it with a wage that started at 85 times the average, and the resulting strings of digits will blow your proletarian mind. And, as was revealed in the cascade of corporate scandals, many of these big fat CEO bonuses and options remained off the company's books, making for a rosier and rounder bottom line, bloated stock prices, and further engorgement of the bonuses.

The argument that defenders of inordinate CEO pay make is that you have to pay the big bucks to get the big boys. A top-performing CEO, like Michaels Jackson and Jordan, is a superstar, and should be remunerated as such. The problem with this argument is that it is difficult to draw any direct correlation between CEO pay and actual performance. If either of the Michaels, Jackson or Jordan, can no longer put the bums in seats, then it's au revoir to the fat checks. Jackson is a good case of this. Now that he is synonymous with noselessness and molestation allegations, his career has evaporated. The boardroom lacks even this modicum of rough justice. There are all too many cases where a CEO screws his company six ways to Sunday and still pulls down the big bucks. The kleptocrats of Enron and WorldCom are the most egregious examples, but the phenomenon is widespread in more legitimate enterprises as well. A report produced by the advocacy group United for a Fair Economy tracked the stock performance of companies with top-paid CEOs over a period of seven years, and its findings give the lie to the link between CEO pay and stock performance. For example, if you invested in Disney the year that

Michael Eisner topped the pay charts, your investment actually eroded over the next year. If you kept reinvesting that money in companies represented by each year's best-paid CEO, your investment continued to decline. According to the United for a Fair Economy estimates, an initial investment of $10,000 in companies with the highest-paid CEOs, would have dwindled to a mere $3,500 over the course of the late nineties. Conversely, the same 10,000 clams, invested in the S&P 500 index of stocks over the same period of time, would have grown to about $32,000.

The pay-for-performance argument also loses some force when you check out the severance packages awarded to outgoing CEOs. After years of overly ambitious, terribly expensive expansion in foreign markets, a high-profile, multimillion-dollar racial discrimination lawsuit, reports of contaminated Coke from European bottlers, and a couple of consecutive quarters of net losses, Coca-Cola CEO Douglas Ivester hit the road with a cool 120 million bucks in his back pocket. My favorite quote from the book of Ivester is his devil-may-care response to the European reports of contaminated Coke: "Where the fuck is Belgium?" Coke stocks finally rebounded when Doug Daft, his successor, took the helm in 2000, but not just because Doug the First took a powder; as soon as Daft was hired, he organized a massive restructuring plan, which is, of course, corporatese for firing, and lots of it. Daft sacked 20 percent of Coke's payroll the month after he was hired. Nobody mourned the passing of the age of Doug the First. In fact, a middle manager culled in the bulk firings said, "The mood is pretty lousy, but this shake-up was long overdue." Stockholm syndrome is one way of coping with a pink slip.

The truly disturbing thing about the Coke case is that it is the rule, not the exception. The CEOs with the five fattest paychecks in 1999 all fired more than a thousand people, or at least 5 percent of their employees. Since labor is generally the largest fixed cost for any corporation, CEOs discovered that they could achieve a nice little bounce in their stock prices, and consequently their bonuses, by downsizing aggressively. The speculative economy, once a way of raising capital for productive ventures, began cannibalizing the productive economy.

In the business press, the phrase *a commitment to productivity* has gradually come to mean a commitment to getting rid of the people who produce things. As GE CEO "Neutron" Jack Welch once said, "Strong managers who make tough decisions to cut jobs provide the only job security in today's world." It's not just that people like Welch are willing to slash hundreds of thousands of jobs, export work to countries with nineteenth-century labor laws, and destroy years of union advocacy for well-paid work. They also have the nerve to insist that getting rid of good jobs somehow magically creates job security. If Jack Welch was your boss, how secure would you feel knowing that the grand poobah has nary a qualm about firing tens of thousands of people at a shot? Nevertheless, the business press hails him as a managerial genius, and credits him with GE's phenomenal market growth.

When I first began writing this book, Jack Welch was riding high, with an autobiography, *Straight from the Gut,* on the *New York Times* best-seller list. Granted, he did retire from GE earlier than planned, in September of 2001, after European regulators refused to allow GE to acquire Honeywell, but his retirement elicited heaps of laudatory eulogies. Since then, though, GE has been accused of using overly aggressive accounting measures under Welch's reign. He also went through a highly publicized divorce in the wake of his highly publicized affair with a former editor from the *Harvard Business Review*. She went to interview him for a profile, and the rest, as they say, is adultery. Though Jack and Jane Welch reached an out-of-court settlement before their divorce went to trial, the court papers provided the press with another peek at the lavish world of CEO perks. After he retired, Welch still had the use of an $80,000-per-month apartment in Manhattan, where his needs for food, flowers, laundry, and wine were tended to by GE. Welch also had the use of company luxury vehicles, season tickets to sporting events, and jaunts on the company Gulf-stream. Bear in mind that when Mr. Welch left GE, his personal fortune was an estimated $900 million. I think the dude can spring for his own roses, but these sorts of perks are de rigueur for the imperial CEO, and evidence that we live in an Oscar gift bag world, where those who have the most get the most for free.

The fact that there is a direct correlation between mass firings and gross prosperity for the fortunate few is not just unfair, is not merely bullshit; it's also unsustainable. There is no cost savings to the company when you follow up your mega-downsizing with obscene bonuses for the people on top. Instead of giving the millions to hundreds of people, to spread around their respective communities, this gives those same millions to a handful of old white guys who already have millions. Down at the economic bottom, job security becomes a distant memory, an artifact or antique. Nobody expects to sign up at Imperial Widgets and stay until retirement with a gold watch and a decent pension anymore. The manufacturing sector in North America has been eviscerated because capital can pull up stakes, relocate to the Third World to sun itself, excrete wherever it pleases, and pay desperately poor people pennies a day to produce the glorious things we so desperately crave.

The death of manufacturing has problematic side effects, inasmuch as manufacturing jobs have a higher economic multiplier effect than the low-paid grunt work of the service industry. The biggest employers in the U.S. used to be manufacturing concerns, like the old GE, which paid people a living wage. Now the biggest bosses are Manpower, provider of temp employment to the masses, and Wal-Mart. And even though the smocks that Wal-Mart employees wear proudly proclaim that "Our People Make the Difference!", the nice people who work there receive wages just above the legal minimum. Moreover, the behemoths of the service sector are notorious for defining a "full-time" work week as twenty-eight to thirty-five hours, thus disqualifying their employees for goodies that were the rule in old-school manufacturing jobs, like benefits and health coverage. This means some people need to get two shitty jobs, and work fifty or sixty hours a week, to try to approximate a living wage. Herd someone out of their forty hours a week at twenty dollars an hour, and into sixty hours at six bucks an hour, and voilà—increased productivity!

When I was a kid, I had a revelation about that most economical of family entertainments, the board game Monopoly. I realized that they sold packages of Monopoly money at the mall near my house. My brother finally figured out my cunning little scheme after a couple of devastating losses to the Billionaire of Baltic Place. Cheating? *Moi? Au contraire, mon frère!* It takes money to make money, and I had merely invested the capital of my allowance in a speculative venture. Similarly, the CEOs of the boom realized that they were sitting on tons of money in worker pay, money that could be transformed, miraculously, into profits, by cutting labor costs. But firing people to boost a profit margin doesn't make a CEO a "top performer" any more than an extra pack of brightly colored bills makes me a Monopoly champ.

Stock ideally represents a share of a company's assets and profits. But the fact that stock rises—and its owners along with it—in the wake of mass firings says more about what corporations consider an asset than a million mealymouthed Human Resources brochures and Wal-Mart smocks. Incomes might have increased over the past twenty years, but real wages for average workers have held steady or declined. The so-called boom served only to exacerbate income inequality trends that have been at work in North America since the eighties. Between 1979 and 2000, the income growth for those in the top 1 percent of income earners increased by 201 percent, while those in the middle quintile enjoyed an increase of 15 percent, and the lowest quintile made a paltry 8 percent gain. Bragging about a substantive increase in the U.S. median income is a case of lies, damned lies, and statistics. When you add up the wildly inflated incomes of the wealthiest percentiles, and everyone else, you get averages that sound nice, but that fail to account for the growing disparity in income. Factor in increased costs for necessities like housing, health care, and education, and the situation looks even grimmer.

Part of the problem with economic statistics is that they are statistics—blunt approximations of the way people live. For example, that 6 percent unemployment rate doesn't sound so catastrophic, does it? It seems okay until you think about the fact that the terminally unemployable don't show up in the statistics, since they are no longer looking for work. Hundreds of thousands of these people fell off the rolls throughout the supposed recovery. And when you factor in the underemployed, who don't get enough hours, or don't get paid enough for the hours they do get, the numbers are not so swell. *The Atlantic Monthly,* which adjusted the figures for part-time and minimum-wage work, estimated that there were actually 21 million underemployed, not 7 million. And even that figure doesn't account for an entire incarcerated underclass, the millions crammed in the big houses of jail-crazy America.

During the last long boom, the one that ran throughout the sixties, average wages increased across the board. This was due in part to growth in sectors that offered steady, well-paid work, such as manufacturing and civil service. But since the 1980s, both of these sectors have been in decline, and have been supplanted by the more polarized wage scale of the service industry. When my pops and his pals graduated from high school and were ready to enter the workforce, they had few problems finding steady work at the shipyard or the plant or on fishing boats. Throw in a couple of super-cheap years of college, and they could teach or join the civil service. By the time I graduated from high school, the shipyard was automated, the plant was on half-time, and the fishing industry was belly up. The government wasn't hiring, either. College was no longer cheap—nor was it optional, since a BA had become the equivalent of a high-school diploma in my dad's day.

The nineties' boom did not look like the last long boom, the real long boom. Wage distribution for that boom looks like a bell curve, with a few people on the bottom and top, and the vast majority falling in the middle. Income inequality actually declined steadily from the postwar period to the seventies. From 1947 until the late seventies, everybody's income, from the lowest quintile to the top five percent, went up. The gains for those at the bottom, the middle, and the top income brackets are comparable, too, at 116 percent, 111 percent, and 86 percent, respectively. But since the 1980s, wealth distribution looks more and more like a flat line, with a sharp vertical spike representing the very rich.

Income gaps have only been exacerbated by recent tax policy. Bush's tax policies are, despite their phony populist veneer, overwhelmingly slanted toward the richest of the rich. Sure, Average Q. Taxpayer has gotten a couple of hundred bucks of his hard-earned dough back from the greedy grasp of the state, but this is chump change compared to the millions in breaks for wealthy individuals and corporations. Even the pragmatics of tax policy favor the wealthy. A front-page story in the *New York Times* noted that the Internal Revenue Service was far more zealous in auditing the working poor than wealthy investors, even though the latter have more to hide and better resources to help them hide it. Bush admitted as much in a campaign town hall session: "Real rich people figure out how to dodge taxes." I guess all those tax breaks, like the war in Iraq, are merely preempting the inevitable.

The growth of income inequality is also the result of a shift in the business of business. The big success stories of the past couple of decades, such as Wal-Mart, are more likely to have a few very highly paid workers (CEOs, etc.), a lot of ill-paid workers (cashiers, sweatshop laborers, etc.), and not a lot in the middle. And even though the stock market went up and up, and productivity kept on rising, wages were never allowed to rise at the same pace, for fear that this would lead to inflation. If the minimum wage had inflated as much as CEO pay or margin debt, cashiers and rib-joint ladies would be making hundreds of dollars an hour.

After the bubble burst, and the boom busted, corporations all over North America cravenly used September 11 as an excuse to fire people by the hundreds of thousands. At the same time, leaders such as Bush and Giuliani insisted that the best thing people could do for New York, and the economy in general, was to shop till they dropped. And though all the yackity-yack about a stimulus package to reboot the troubled economy might have seemed like some Keynesian flashback, Bush's idea of aid takes the form of direct cash transfers and tax credits to some of the wealthiest individuals and corporations in America—the very entities least likely to need, or for that matter, spend them. Call me a crank, but the only things I see trickling down are pink slips and platitudes.

One of the things that help sustain the illusion that there is still a thriving middle class is the increase in consumer debt. People are going into hock to maintain a middle-class lifestyle, racking up thousands in credit card debt, at positively usurious rates. One could argue, in fact, that personal debt has generated the consumer spending that has kept us from spiraling further into recession. Much of this is mortgage refinancing, which means that people are putting their homes on the line in order to overspend—and I suspect there will be beaucoup de foreclosures when interest rates rise above their current record lows. American debt service ratios are holding steady at about 13 percent because the rising worth of real estate and record homeownership have helped offset the growth of debt, but real estate prices cannot rise forever, and interest rates cannot go lower without resorting to negative integers. Depending on usury also helps accelerate the growth of inequality, since credit costs, and does so regressively. The poorer you are, the more expensive it is. Payday lenders, for example, charge triple-digit rates that would embarrass a loan shark. If, however, you are one of the super-rich, then usury is your friend, and one of your primary sources of wealth.

I'm not saying that we should beat our Palm Pilots into

plowshares and go back to the mills. There was nothing inherently magical about digging for coal or working in a car plant. These industries enjoyed better pay and job security thanks to union workers who for years bled in the streets. But union membership is on the wane: The service and retail sectors remain largely untainted by the blight of collective bargaining; and the tech sector, with its 401Ks, encouraged workers to stop thinking of themselves as brother and sister and become shareholders instead. It's been downhill since Reagan told the air traffic controllers to go pound sand. One of market fundamentalism's articles of faith is that unions are awful, and that belief is one thing that *has* managed to trickle down.

How do I know people think unions are bad? Well, brothers and sisters, plenty of people told me as much when, working for a teaching assistants' local, I ran around begging them to please, pretty please, come to the union meeting tonight. Nobody beat me with a lead pipe—this was no old Rockefeller mine. But a few grumbled about wasted dues, and the rest remained indifferent, as though I were trying to get them to come to the chess club or a Tupperware party. Everyone sat around the bar and griped about being broke as shit, but only a handful of folks wanted to get together and mention that fact to our august employers. Most people just didn't see what was in it for them.

The prevailing worldview at grad school seemed to be that you busted your hump to publish as much stuff and get as much funding as you could, scraping by on part-time jobs and loans until the mystical moment around middle age when you got tenure and were set for life, like your profs. But those profs didn't just have the advantage of getting their PhDs at the same time as all that sweet, sweet sixties' government funding.

They also organized and represented themselves. In my grad school, on the other hand, people conducted themselves as individuals in competition, not as members of a class.

This phenomenon isn't limited to grad school: In the high-profile professions that ruled during the boom, Xtreme competition was the rule. Unionization is actively discouraged in the service industry, where employees are encouraged to feel they're part of a team, loyal to the brand and the leadership. Union work became a lazy-Teamster joke, not nearly as cool as Brave New Work—the flex-time telecommunications job with the stock options. And because unions are only as strong as their members, the "unions are bad" idea has become a self-fulfilling prophecy. The less people believe in unions, the less power they have. The less power they have, the less people believe in unions. Without the unions to exert pressure on wages, there's no good reason for employers to raise them, even as all the other economic indicators float up, up, and away.

The boom might have been unprecedented, but it wasn't entirely unfamiliar. The super-rich continued to get super-richer, the moderately rich did well, the middle class lost ground, and the poor were left, to bum a phrase from Donald Barthelme, sucking the mop. Bush dismissed critics of his pro-plutocrat tax giveaway by insisting his detractors were trying to stir up class warfare. And his rhetoric was effective. Most Americans labor under the delusion that they live in a classless society, where such Euro-commie talk does not apply. They cling to the myth of upward mobility, the sense that anyone, if sufficiently blessed with astounding bone structure, a boffo idea, and a willingness to work themselves to the very marrow, can be a billionaire. Since Reagan, who declared that he wanted to live in an America where everyone could be rich, the atmosphere has been more like class bullying than class war, with everyone disdaining their immediate inferiors and aspiring to become their superiors. We labor under the collective misapprehension that we are pre-rich. This is one of the reasons why so many people rushed out and bought stock, and one of the reasons why people continue to vote against their own economic interests. However, despite widespread and contagious delusions of impending wealth, people are less likely to move on up the class ladder than they were before the boom. As income inequality has increased, class mobility has declined. When *The Economist*—hardly a socialist rag—is bemoaning the decline of meritocracy and fretting about a calcifying American class system, as they did in December of 2004, it would appear things have taken a definite turn for the dynastic.

Throughout the ages, there have been choruses of warnings against the corrosive effects of income inequality. You'll find the message in golden oldies like the Bible, Plato's *Republic,* and in Francis Bacon's admonition that wealth is like muck— useless unless you spread it around. Founding Fathers like Jefferson and Madison had strong words about the impact of an excessive income gap on the body politic. For a more timely take, consult the Princeton professor and *New York Times* columnist Paul Krugman, who rightly rails against the Bushies' mendacious math. The U.S. might be home to the majority of the world's billionaires, but using the wealth of the CEOs as a measure of the health and vitality of the economy makes about as much sense as basing crop predictions on the health of the king. The further the rich float into a scrubbed bubble of entitlement, and the longer the less-than-rich are left to seethe under a heap of debt and resentment, the worse this joint gets for each and every one of us.

Which would you rather have, an enclave of fantastically wealthy CEOs, enjoying a lifestyle that makes Versailles look like a rustic commune, or good schools, good health care, and a living wage? This is a choice that the government is currently making on your behalf, and they've picked the billionaires every time, no matter how platitudinous they wax about leaving no child behind. Did Americans really throw off the yoke of English tyranny so they could bow down to a set of new kings—monarchs of Mammon like those self-lavishing cheats Dennis Kozlowski, Jack Welch, and Ken Lay?

CHAPTER FOUR

WORLD CO., INC.

Artificial People Power

*When abuses like this begin to surface in the corporate
world, it is time to reaffirm the basic principles and rules
that make capitalism work: truthful books and honest
people, and well-enforced laws against fraud and
corruption. All investment is an act of faith, and faith is
earned by integrity. In the long run, there's no capitalism
without conscience; there is no wealth without character.*

PRESIDENT GEORGE W. BUSH

When booms go bust, they tend to flush out companies
that have, in the giddy spirit of bullish excess, been less
than forthright about their books. The last bust was no exception. The Enron scandal, the ur-fraud, began coming to public
consciousness in fall 2001, and Enron declared bankruptcy by
December. That was the biggest such bankruptcy ever until
July of 2002, when WorldCom finally tumbled into its own
fantastic imploding sinkhole. Those two remain the heavy-
weight champions of corporate fraud, but throughout 2002
and 2003, a wave of lesser corporate scandals, from Adelphia
to Xerox, revealed "accounting irregularities" in the billions of

dollars. "Accounting irregularities" is North American euphemese for senior executives and their chums on the board
contriving utterly bogus financial statements, swindling their
shareholders, employees, and the public, and absconding with
millions and millions of dollars. Marketeers were quick to
characterize the collapse of these behemoths of bullshit as the
market correcting its own excesses, outing the truth in its
inimitable market way. "Companies come and go. It's part of
the genius of capitalism," enthused Paul O' Neill, the then secretary of the Treasury.

Apparently, the two biggest bankruptcies in American history weren't a sign of systemic rot but proof that the system
worked. And while it is true that a shift in the business cycle
was partially responsible for outing some of the more spectac-
ular instances of corporate fraud, the greater share of the
credit and blame belong to whistleblowers and sheer hubris
on the part of the perpetrators. The market let all that shit
happen for a long damn time before the genius of capitalism
kicked in.

The suits also attempted to minimize the radius of corruption. The "one bad apple don't spoil the whole bunch" cliché
got a lot of play, as politicians, analysts, and commentators
tried to ward off the creeping Enronitis. Most companies, we
were told, were as honest and true as the family pooch. We
needn't get all worked up into a regulatory lather over the few
bad apples. And please, pretty please, Mr. and Mrs. John Q.
Public, keep those investment dollars flowing. No investor
confidence crisis here, folks.

The bad apple cliché is off on a couple of counts. When we
are talking about corporate scandals, we aren't talking about a
few piddly little Granny Smiths. Companies like WorldCom
and Enron were among the planet's hugest, most high-profile

concerns, in big-deal fields like telecommunications and energy. The taint of scandal isn't confined to a couple of excessively effusive companies, either. Executives at Tyco, Waste Management, Qwest Communications, Global Crossing, ImClone, Tenet Health, HealthSouth, and Vivendi have also been accused of various forms of malfeasance. Accounting firms such as Arthur Andersen were implicated in the divers scandals, as were major investment banks, such as Citigroup and Merrill Lynch. Major players in mutual fund and insurance industries are also under current investigation by the SEC and New York Attorney General Eliot Spitzer.

These corporate scandals are hardly proof that the system works. Rather, the failure of so many so-called checks and balances tells us that we have serious corporate governance issues. Corporations have long insisted that they be allowed to govern themselves as they see fit, and have been bridling under the yoke of government regulation. They are still perfectly happy to cash government checks, and hand bales of dough to politicians willing to push the deregulation agenda, but they don't like it when the government gets bossy or nosy. The business community argues that they have their own self-regulating mechanisms, like auditors, accountants, analysts, credit bureaus, corporate boards, and the sainted market itself, à la the raptures of O'Neill. All of these self-regulating mechanisms failed in the case of the corporate crime wave.

The watchdogs were far too busy chewing on juicy steaks to bark. Auditors who were supposed to scrutinize the numbers were also busy consulting, which is to say, cooking up creative numbers and creating artful dodges for their clients. According to the Securities Exchange Commission, half of the accounting firms' revenue in 2000 came from consulting, as opposed to a piffling 13 percent in 1981. At the banks, analysts

who were supposed to recommend prudent buys instead rec-
ommended just about everything to a stock-crazed populace.
The corporate board members, supposedly there to protect
the interests of the shareholders, aided and abetted the fictions
of the CEOs who, more likely than not, selected them to sit on
the boards in the first place.

There is a delightful term for the latter phenomenon—incestuous affirmation. Incestuous affirmation sets in when one
grows so powerful and wealthy that one is utterly isolated from
anyone but the like-minded or toadying. Examples of the deleterious effects of incestuous affirmation include Donald
Trump's hair, Michael Jackson's face, and the Bush war cabinet.
Another prime example of this phenomenon is Conrad Black,
who used his company, Hollinger International, as a personal
piggy bank for years thanks to a board disinclined to notice, let
alone censure him for it. The board finally snapped to and gave
Black the boot in November 2003, and the SEC charged Black,
his COO, and Hollinger with fraud in November of 2004.

Everyone knows that corporate crime is nice work if you
can get it, much more lucrative and low-risk than other, more
vulgar, forms of law-breaking. Forget all those right-wrong
questions and do the cost-benefit analysis. Corporate crime
pays. But those purloined millions didn't come from some
fantastic infinite market force. Corporate criminals made their
millions the old-fashioned way: They stole them. They elided
the public purse. Nothing washes down a little off-book profiteering like setting up dozens of offshore tax shelters. They
milked and bilked the public purse, too, benefiting from
sweetheart deals and custom-made legislation. They bor-
rowed themselves blind, and then recorded the loans as
though they were profits. They shafted millions of customers,
as evidenced by California's rolling blackouts, to name but one

example of price-gouging and crappy service. The employees of corrupt concerns also got royally screwed. They weren't just out of jobs when the company crashed and burned. Many also lost the savings they had invested.

Employees, pension fund administrators, institutional investors, and shareholders freaked out with each new crest in the corporate crime wave, and rightly so. Why, it got so bad that Bush had to stage a crackdown on this sort of thing, particularly with the press speculating about the admin's very cozy relationship with persons of interest such as Ken "Kenny-Boy" Lay. In July of 2002, shortly after WorldCom began to implode, Bush announced the creation of the Corporate Responsibility Task Force, a "financial-crime SWAT team," wholly and solely devoted to the pursuit of white-collar evildoers. He furrowed his brow, chastised the chiselers and book-cookers, blustered about trust and transparency, and swore he would bring the crooked businesspeople to justice.

Larry Thompson, a Department of Justice official, headed up the task force. Before Thompson joined the Department of Justice in 2001, he spent a few years on the board at Providian, a credit card company that paid hundreds of millions of dollars to settle suits for allegations of securities and consumer fraud, while, of course, denying all wrongdoing. They paid up, but would not confirm or deny the allegations. Thompson supporters insisted that he had been a force for rectitude when dealing with the fraud fallout at Providian, but it became a moot point, anyway, since Larry didn't last that long. The most recent update of the Corporate Responsibility Web page on the White House site is a one-year anniversary press release, from July of 2003, boasting of a couple of hundred charges filed. Larry decamped in August of 2003, and I haven't heard or read thing one about his replacement in the mainstream press.

The task force did issue one other press release, celebrating their second anniversary in 2004, but I had to go to LexisNexis to dig it up. This press release claims the SWAT team was responsible for more than five hundred convictions or guilty pleas, including thirty-one charges for those involved in the Enron scandal. The task force is also proud of the part it played in the corporate cases that have come to trial thus far, like the Adelphia, Martha Stewart, and Frank Quattrone trials. Of course, in the case of both Martha Stewart, the SEC's conveniently famous scapegoat, and venture capitalist Quattrone, the charges were actually obstruction of justice charges. And even though it is easier to prosecute a cover-up than a complex fraud scheme, which is precisely why they were charged with obstruction instead of insider trading or fraud, Martha got a piffling five months in the hoosegow and Quattrone's first trial ended in a hung jury. The Adelphia case was also declared a mistrial.

It should also be noted that the tasking of the force did not involve much in the way of new funds, or new personnel, and was instead a coordination of existing resources in the FBI, SEC, IRS, and DOJ. Some involved in the corporate crime investigations have complained that the demands of the War on Terror have siphoned away resources and experienced agents. The most vigorous pursuer of corporate criminals, in terms of high-profile settlements and suits, is not the Corporate Responsibility Task Force, but New York State Attorney General Eliot Spitzer, who has successfully taken on megabanks, mutual funds, and insurers. I am quite sure you have heard of the tenacious Mr. Spitzer. I am equally sure you have not heard of James B. Comey, the head of the Corporate Responsibility Task Force as of that 2004 press release.

Even though there are some corporate crooks who have already been sentenced, like Enron's Andrew Fastow, the really huge trials, the Ken Lay trial, and the HealthSouth trial, wait in the wings, and will take place over the course of 2005. Bernie Ebbers of WorldCom was convicted in March 2005. His "aw-shucks" defense didn't work. The Tyco and Adelphia retrials are in the pipe, too, following a go-round of mistrials. It seems that juries do not particularly enjoy parsing sophisticated accounting schemes, and they are not especially adept in the arcane fiscal arts. It remains to be seen how severely the justice system will punish these alleged malefactors of great wealth, but most of them are marching into court under the banner of Not Guilty.

On the legislative side, the Sarbanes-Oxley Act became law shortly after Bush announced his corporate crime crackdown. Democratic senator Paul Sarbanes initially floated the bill, to furious objections from Republicans. Republican senator Michael Oxley, a beneficiary of donations from the investment community, was against the bill before he co-sponsored it. Both sides haggled their way to a compromise when they saw something needed to be done, or—to be perfectly cynical— when they realized they could get more political capital from a crackdown than from the appearance of condoning these shenanigans to the point of complicity. A defanged version of the original bill eventually passed the House and the Senate by resounding majorities. Provisions of the bipartisan bill include the creation of an accounting oversight board, the requirement that top company officers sign off on all financial statements, and stricter penalties and longer sentences for white-collar crimes.

These measures are steps in the right direction, but I have to admit the signing rules come as something of a surprise. I have to sign the back of a $40 Christmas check from my grandma, but the head of an enormous multimillion-dollar concern *doesn't* need to sign off on company financial statements? Suffice it to say that I'm glad they got around to fixing that. However, the legislation does have a few notable omissions. There is nothing in the legislation about off-book bonus expensing, for example, which was one of the problems common to most corporate scandals. Republican Phil Gramm even went so far as to say that government messing with this kind of accounting would be "very dangerous and very counterproductive." It may come as no surprise that Gramm and his wife have been members of a number of corporate boards, including Enron's. Furthermore, the first choice to lead the oversight board, pension administrator John H. Biggs, was scuttled by the Republicans, and Harvey Pitt at the SEC, because they thought he was too tough on business. The corporate community is none too pleased about the costs and paperwork involved with Sarbanes-Oxley compliance, which has become a multimillion-dollar growth industry in itself. The Web teems with Sarbanes-Oxley software and consultation services. It has been a super-sweet couple of years for accounting firms, particularly the big ones, which is pretty funny when you consider their culpability in creating the problem in the first place. It's the genius of capitalism!

Measures like longer jail terms for corporate crime, or securing executive autographs, salutary though they may be, are like Band-Aids on cancer. They fail to address the more fundamental problems with crony capitalism, and its major institution, the corporation.

Let us start with the fallacy that serves as the foundation for over a century of corporate law. In the eyes of the law, corporations are people, legally no different from you or your grandma.

You can't kick or kiss or kill one of these artificial people, but they nevertheless enjoy people-style blandishments, like free speech rights, property rights, protection from search and seizure, and access to credit, with few of the attendant hassles of being human, like disease and hunger. You see, corporations are magical, mystical things, people and not-people, deathless and everywhere. It's enough to make a gal burst into Seussian song! Oh, the things you could do, if you were a corporation! The places you'd go! The money you'd make! Being horribly real and terribly fake!

Corporations sprung up in Europe in the fifteenth century as a way of gathering funds for colonial forays to the New Worlds. The first companies—like the British and Dutch East India Companies and the still-going Hudson's Bay Company—were formed in the 1600s and 1700s to raise enough capital to found colonies and expand international trade. Chartered by monarchs, they were the precursors to today's multinationals. Some of the American colonies themselves, like the settlements in Virginia and New England, started as just this kind of corporate endeavor. The Boston Tea Party, one of the great set pieces of America's fight for independence, was as much a cri de coeur against corporate as colonial rule. The rebels didn't like the king and his stinking taxes, but they had no kind words for the unfair market practices of the East India Company, either. The caffeinated beverages hurled, the rebellion against the Man—it was like the battle in Seattle before there, like, was a Seattle, man.

There were no provisions in the founding American documents about granting charters to corporations. Thomas Jefferson feared that national chartering would encourage the growth of monopolies, which he saw as one of the great threats to human liberty. Consequently, only one federal charter was granted, to the Bank of North America, in 1781. This charter was revoked in the 1800s, due to charges of corruption, and a Second Bank formed. This bank and its sequel were the exception to the rule. The vast majority of corporations were chartered by individual states, which pursued this task with varying zeal. Some states put it to a vote in their legislatures, and others, particularly if the organization in question was a bank, put it to their voters.

Through the first half of the 1800s, the state charters demanded that corporations follow rules for the privilege of incorporation; a company had to have an express purpose, and was limited in its land and capital holdings, and the charters were legit only for a decade or two. Most corporate charters involved a finite goal, like building a bridge, and the corporate entity dissolved when the project was completed. Corporations were not permitted to hold stock in other corporations, to prevent the formation of powerful conglomerates. Some states, like Wyoming and California, had extensive lists of requirements for corporations seeking charters. Pennsylvania expressly forbade corporate endeavors that were injurious to the citizens of the commonwealth. Others, like New Jersey and Delaware, used lax rules and simpler registration processes to lure businesses away from the sticklers. Delaware's lax laws continue to attract a boisterous population of corporate citizens. More than half of the companies listed in the Fortune 500 are incorporated in the itsy-bitsy state.

For most of the 1800s, corporations were viewed as creations of the law that were subject to the law, subordinate to the state and the citizens. Corporate lawyers tried, throughout the century, to argue against the limited powers provided by corporate charters and win more extensive rights for their increasingly moneyed masters. The Civil War marked a crucial turning point in favor of corporate rights, as war profits gave companies the wherewithal to exploit an unstable political and legal climate to their own advantage. Corporations started becoming people in 1886, with the U.S. Supreme Court's ruling in the case of *Santa Clara County vs. Southern Pacific Railroad.* This decision decreed that corporations were persons and consequently enjoyed the protection of the Fourteenth Amendment.

This ruling became the cornerstone of corporate law throughout the Gilded Age. Even though the Fourteenth Amendment is traditionally associated with the end of slavery, corporate lawyers were the ones who invoked it most. After the *Santa Clara* decision, 288 corporate cases made their way through the courts, versus 19 civil rights cases. Subsequent decisions granted even more rights to corporations based on this assumption that they were people. In the 1893 case of *Noble vs. Union River Logging,* the court ruled that corporations also enjoyed the protection of the Bill of Rights. In the 1906 case of *Hale vs. Henkel,* the court ruled that corporations enjoyed the protection of the Fourth Amendment, meaning they could not be searched or seized. In the 1922 case of *Pennsylvania Coal Company vs. Mahon,* the court ruled that corporations enjoyed the protection of the Fifth Amendment, particularly the "takings" clause, which stresses that no private good may be taken by the government without just compensation.

In Britain, corporations had been considered "artificial persons" for quite some time. But the intent of the British law was regulatory; corporations were persons in that they could sue or be sued and be prosecuted for breaking laws that began with the clause *no person shall.* The *Santa Clara* decision was different. It put corporations on track for all the rights that citizens enjoy, including protection against search or seizure and the right to free speech. As the artificial people grew increasingly autonomous, the real people who ran the artificial people became less liable and culpable for anything the artificial people might happen to do. The states were supposed to hold these artificial people accountable, but of late, they have sat on their hands. There are no longer restrictions on capital or land ownership; there are no more demands that the corporation fulfill a specific purpose, other than profit by any means necessary. Though there is a lovely Latin term in corporate law, *ultra vires,* beyond men, that refers to actions beyond the power granted by the corporate charter, the corporate chartering process today sets few limits on artificial-people power.

State attorney generals still have the authority to revoke corporate charters, and there have been grassroots rumblings about revoking the state charters of offending corporations—major polluters, for example—in California. But the fact that this notion remains the stuff of lefty rallies demonstrates that states are unwilling to flex their muscle. This would be the artificial person equivalent to being executed by the state, and in the U.S., they like to save that sort of thing for real people.

Instead, the financially strapped states are perpetually engaged in a race to attract corporate investment, and sound more and more like furniture barons in the throes of faked demise: "Everything must go!" They happily hand out tasty tax breaks and incentive packages for the promise of jobs. The rationale? You can't be a stickler, these days. Nobody likes a stickler, and there are plenty of pliant poor people of varying hues scattered all over the globe who aren't as persnickety about labor laws. NAFTA has made it a breeze to move operations to a sweatshop in China or a Mexican maquiladora. The balance of power has shifted. Companies no longer court or found communities. Instead, communities beg companies to grace their towns, and pimp themselves out with ads about nonqualities like excellence and diversity, or offer bribes in the form of tax breaks, subsidies, and cheap labor.

Recognizing corporations as people was a contrivance of the law to make corporations subject to law without crushing the spirit of enterprise. Limited liability allows people to try new things. Punitive liability—early incorporators were personally liable, and in some cases, doubly and trebly so, for debts incurred by a corporation—was a hindrance to free enterprise. If your soapworks could land you in debtor's prison, you'd be less inclined to get the operation up and running. It may have been awfully accountable, but it sure as hell wasn't an incentive. The problem with the hindrance-to-free-enterprise argument is that it has been reiterated so frequently over the past century. Pollution control? *Hindrance.* Labor laws? *Hindrance.* Antitrust laws? *Hindrance.* Any attempt on the part of states to regulate corporate activity is now painted as protectionism or as interference with the supreme wisdom of the market.

Real people are subject to regulation. We enjoy a great deal of freedom in North America, but certain things are simply not done. The no-nos in your head, the cop working the beat in your brain, is what puts the civil in civil society. You can't steal, then expect your own property to be waiting for you at home. You can't relieve yourself on your neighbor's welcome mat. You can't punch people for dressing badly, and so on. Life under democracy is equal parts personal space and the Golden Rule—don't bother me, and I won't bother you. Self-interest as the high road to freedom is not new, by any means. It is there in the pursuit of happiness clause of the Declaration of Independence, and it is there in Adam Smith's insistence that we build a social order that makes a good of our vices, like greed, instead of appealing to our virtues. But Enlightenment thinkers like Smith and the Founding Fathers recognized that the boundary of self-interest is someone else's self-interest and the universal self-interest of every free person. Your pursuit of happiness couldn't run roughshod over someone else's, since both of you enjoyed the equal protection of the law.

Consider that classic economic chestnut about the division and specialization of labor, Adam Smith's pin factory example. The cool thing about Smith's pin factory wasn't just that it made more pins, thus fattening the CEO of Pin Inc. The pin factory made better pins, and made life easier for pin makers and pin users, thus fulfilling the self-interest of the majority. While Smith was an ardent advocate of free trade, marketeers cherry-pick his writings to justify practices that would have made the Scottish moral philosopher recoil in horror. One of the primary ethical ideas of the Enlightenment was Immanuel Kant's categorical imperative: "Act so that your maxim might be the object of a universal law." Or, *don't do anything you wouldn't want everyone else to do.* This seems sadly quaint, less au courant than the catalog imperative, *you are what you buy,* or bullshit imperatives like *everybody else is doing it, I didn't realize it was wrong,* or *I do not recall.*

Both corporations and actual people are self-interested entities. This is a Well, Duh proposition. Even those companies that offer free lunches to the urchins or plant new trees to replenish the foliage they devour still try to be good and look good in order to gain a larger market share or maintain existing business. The problem with the implied equality between real people and their artificial corporate friends is a significant difference in the way the two express their respective self-interest. The prevailing self-interest of a real person is life. The prevailing self-interest of an artificial person is profit. The two-legged guys come and go, talking of mergers and escrow, but the artificial person, the Coca-Cola corporation, lives for more than a hundred years with no signs of senility or reduced mobility. And even though pretty much everybody on the planet knows that Coca-Cola guy, few and far between are those who could name the wizards behind the curtain of the Coca-Cola guy. Most people can name a few star CEOs in blips like something off a set of Great Suits trading cards; Lee Iacocca, General Motors. Bill Gates, Microsoft. DeLorean . . . DeLorean—car guy—was he the cokehead or the crooked trader? Colorful nicknames help: "Neutron" Jack (Welch), "Chainsaw" Al (Dunlap). But do not confuse the artificial with the real. The real people would be the first to insist, particularly in the event of a hefty lawsuit, that they shouldn't be confused with the artificial people they animate and lead.

It seems to me that a child, let alone the combined brains of government, business, and law, can recognize that there is something fundamentally different about a person and a corporation. Put it to the *Sesame Street* "One of These Things Is Not Like the Other" test in front of a group of toddlers— they'd know the difference. "Here's Fred. Here's Lateesha. Here's Enrique. Here's the corporate headquarters of General Motors. One of these things is not quite the same . . . now it's time to play our game!"

Corporations aren't merely equal to people anymore. While there are some folks, like Bill Gates, who are so wealthy that they have ascended to the commanding heights of corporatification, most people are far, far less powerful than the corporations that surround, sustain, and employ them. Corporations have powers no mere mortal can possess. They have become artificial immortal people who can appear in different parts of the globe simultaneously, like vampires or gods. Ask yourself a couple of questions: Would the government pay *me* wads of money to move to another state, or another country? Can *I* keep gallons and gallons of toxic shit in my yard? Can *I* make a billion dollars and still receive a tax rebate check worth millions? Do I and my team of lobbyists and lawyers regularly enjoy face time with politicians? If the answer to these questions is yes, you may be a corporation. If the answer is no, then you are all too human. I mean, can you fire ten thousand people? God, that would take a long time. Think of how far you'd have to go to scrounge up that many people to can. If you were fair, and only fired the slackers, it could take you years to hand out all those pink slips. And you'd get so sick of the sad faces, having to look them in the eyes and say sorry over and over again. But under the umbrella of the corporation, you and your colleagues could slap together the restructuring plan on the plane, bounce it around in a board meeting, write up the press release, send the word down the line to managers you barely know, and let them say sorry to people you've never even seen. And then you can watch as your stock goes up, and your bank account swells, thanks to your brave decision to downsize, cutting labor costs, increasing productivity, and generating shareholder value.

The difference in powers enjoyed by real people and their artificial coevals is vast, and it continues to grow. It is crazy talk to consider them the same in the eyes of the law. People range in size from midgets to giants, a difference of a few feet and a couple of hundred pounds at the most. Corporations, on the other hand, range from the corner store to behemoths like Wal-Mart. They live longer than people, have more money than people, and are so very much bigger than people that personhood no longer seems like a sufficient or accurate descriptor. The fact that half of the world's biggest economies are corporations puts them in a different league than people.

This is, admittedly, an oft-disputed comparison. Lefties contend that it accurately reflects the fact that a Wal-Mart is closer to a midsized nation like Denmark than it is to a single citizen of any nation, and that there are a number of poor countries whose pitiful GDPs are dwarfed by the revenues of even the minor major corporations. Market boosters, like the nice people at *The Economist,* insist that the figure is an apples and oranges comparison, since it compares GDPs, or what a country produces, to total corporate revenues, or what a company sells, without considering other assets and costs. But while the notion that half of the world's big economies are corporations is subject to debate, it is blatantly obvious that a Wal-Mart or a General Electric is more like a state than a citizen, and involves a lot of people and power rather than just the one legal guy.

This is not merely a question of size. It is also a question of access to state power. Corporations and states are no longer each other's antagonists. I believe the more appropriate adjective for their relationship is *cozy.* And all those warm fuzzies mean that there really isn't anyone working the door. It would be folly to expect corporations to check themselves before they wreck themselves, as Ice Cube advised. Governments used to serve as a countervailing force against corporate power. Through taxation and regulation, they protected the interests of the citizenry against the inordinate growth of artificial-people power. Americans may have perfected the art of creating corporations, but early presidents feared their growing influence, and saw them as a competitor with the republic for power over the people.

This presumption of rivalry has gone the way of the musket and the stovepipe hat. The ludicrously pro-business policies of the past few presidents stand in sharp contrast to the words of earlier presidents. Jefferson wasn't taking any shit from the bankers: He writes in an 1816 letter, "I hope we shall crush in its birth the aristocracy of our moneyed corporations, which dare already to challenge our government to a trial of strength and bid defiance to the laws of our country." Twoscore and five years later, that commie Lincoln said, "Labor is prior to, and independent of, capital. Capital is only the fruit of labor, and could never have existed if labor had not first existed. Labor is the superior of capital, and deserves much the higher consideration."

After the Depression, FDR was of the opinion that big business hadn't held up their end of the deal, and chastised the financial class, declaring that they had failed even on their own terms. "We have always known that heedless self-interest was bad morals," he said, "we now know that it is bad economics." Doesn't that sound like a breath of fresh air? Wouldn't you, just once, love to hear a president chew out a business that blew a wad of private and public money and went bust, instead of simply helping them up, dusting them off, and writing them a check?

The past twenty years have seen a veritable orgy of industry deregulation and breaks for corporations. If you think of corporate personhood as a Pinocchio story, the election of Ronald Reagan marks the point where the Blue Fairy finally makes the wooden puppet a real boy. Reagan did deal with the old antagonism between big business and the state, but he was pitching for the other team and helped inaugurate the absurdity that is anti-government governance. He summed up the previous governments' view of the economy thus: "If it moves, tax it. If it keeps moving, regulate it. And if it stops moving, subsidize it." Reagan insisted he would change this, and change two out of three he did. Businesses paid less tax and faced less strict regulations, but they didn't have to worry about missing out on the rich, creamy subsidies. This was particularly so with favored industries like defense, aerospace, and energy.

Bush the Elder dismissed Reagan's supply-side blend of heavy defense spending, reduced taxation, and attempts to balance the budget as "voodoo economics" before he joined the ticket, but proved to be a manipulator of the old chicken entrails himself once he was installed in office. His most fiscally responsible action, raising tax rates, got him booted out of office, even though it was a significant factor in the government surpluses during the Clinton administration. Those surpluses have, of course, gone down the drain, under the reign of the most corporate-friendly president of them all. Corporate tax revenues as a percentage of all tax revenues have been decreasing under Bush. According to Treasury Department figures, they fell 36 percent between 2000 and 2003, from $207 billion to $132 billion. Then, a couple of weeks before the election, Bush and the gang wrapped up their first term by passing another corporate tax cut package worth an estimated $143 billion.

Even the previously blithe Treasury Secretary, Paul O'Neill, grew less sanguine about the administration's pro-rich, pro-corporate policies. He repeatedly warned Bush that his proposed tax cuts were fiscally irresponsible, and would lead to huge deficits. Cheney dismissed O'Neill's fussing and fretting: "After Reagan, deficits don't matter anymore," quoth the vice prez. By December of 2002, O'Neill was asked to resign. In his book about his time in the inner circle, *The Price of Loyalty,* he describes the intransigent president as "a deaf man in a room full of blind people." Whether or not you agree with that withering assessment, the fact remains that the president has always been a rich man in a room full of rich people.

The collapse of companies like Enron and WorldCom says more than I can about corporate power, and the perils of too many prevailing trends. All the typical bullshit is there: the emphasis on speculation and accounting gimmickry rather than production, the morbidly obese CEO bonuses, the disastrous effects of rapid telecom and energy deregulation, the cozy political connections, the contracts and tax breaks, the cooked books, the 401K retirement funds disappearing as loyal employees get dismissed over the phone or are given thirty minutes to pack up and leave. This is what happens when states allow corporations to do as they wish, and to flout the laws of the land. This is what happens when bullshit artists are allowed to flourish, their phony empires unimpeded by regulation or scrutiny. They certainly weren't scrutinizing themselves, and seemed utterly enthralled with their own feats of bullshit artistry. *The New York Times* ran a lovely photo of the paperweights management used to hand out to Enron employees. They were smooth polished rocks emblazoned with the corporate logo and the word *Integrity,* which introduces the possibility of a deliciously ironic stoning in lieu of jail time.

The corporation is a wonderful way to privatize vast amounts of wealth, while externalizing factors like labor costs, production costs, and costs for raw materials. Externalizing is biz-school speak for making someone else pay, and that's what corporations do every time they leave a big smelly mess for citizens and taxpayers to clean up and sort out, be that in the form of GE dumping PCBs in the Hudson or the financial fallout of the WorldCom bankruptcy filing. Call me old-school, call me paleo-Pennsylvanian, but the appalling behavior of a number of corporate persons makes a little of that antiquated "injurious to the citizens" clause sound pretty good to me. I'm glad to be living among the glorious bounty that corporations have cranked out, of course, but I hardly think it traitorous for us, the real, to say something like, could we please cut it out with the poo puddles, mass firings, insulting wages, denial of benefits, rampant profiteering, flagrant tax evasion, and floods of brain-, white-, and hogwash?

If you find this request impertinent, if it offends your free-market loyalties, just think of how lousy your neighborhood would be if all the real people started doing the kinds of things artificial people get away with. Put it to the Kant test. What if everyone did it? What if everyone behaved like the artificial people? Would it kill 'em to pay their fair share and clean up after themselves? That's the least we ask of real people. Why don't we demand it from the artificial people, the world's Ltds and Cos and Incs?

This is one of my vintage gripes. If this bad juju were Scotch, it would be aged to perfection. I grew up in Sydney, Cape Breton, Nova Scotia. If you've heard of Cape Breton, which is about as far east and north as you can go in Canada before you find yourself swimming to Newfoundland, it's probably for one of three reasons. There's the culture thing: maybe you've heard of writer Alistair McLeod, or fiddler Ashley McIsaac. There's the pristine natural beauty of landmarks like the Cabot Trail. And then there's the giant toxic lake of tar in Sydney, arguably the largest open environmental disaster in Canada, a leftover from the long-gone steel industry.

The Sydney Steel Plant is as sad an example of artificial-people power gone horribly awry as one could ever hope to

find. It's a monument to the slow painful death of North
American manufacturing, and the loss of the job security that
went with it. I don't want to romanticize the factory: the work
was dirty and unhealthy. But at least factory workers were well
paid, unlike their coevals in multinational manufacturing
today, and their counterparts in rapidly growing fields like the
service industry. Those good jobs were what justified the
growing puddle of goo; besides, no one really figured out de-
finitively until at least the eighties that industrial shit could
hurt you. Once the jobs started to go, and only the waste remained, we all started to notice it more—not like it's exactly
hidden or anything. In fact, the tar pond is a couple of miles
away from the main mall downtown, which is but a block
away from my old high school, fantastically bad city planning on both counts. Moreover, Sydney was no more forward-
looking with its human wastes than it was with its industrial
ones. All that went, and continues to go, straight into the harbor. A network of creeks and brooks runs throughout downtown, connecting the harbor, the ponds in the park, and the
great big lake of toxic tar. For some strange reason, Sydney's
cancer and unemployment rates are higher than the national
average.

I haven't even gotten to the insane part yet, which is that
governments have thrown millions and millions of dollars at
the mess, either trying to keep the dying corp up and running,
or whoring for new industries. If they had pitched all the
money straight into the pond, it would have been plugged up,
if not cleaned up, a long time ago. My father particularly sa-
vored the tale of Hustler Industries (I kid you not). They got
an incentive package from the government and the jobs lasted
less than a year before the board of directors cried bankrupt
and bailed, like so many other less aptly named ventures.

WORLD CO., INC.   89

If you want to see what years of corporate mismanagement and government waste look like, hie thee to the thumping heart of downtown Sydney. Gaze out upon that great big gross lake of deadly goo. Given the current state of the cleanup plan, which nobody wants to pay for, it should be there for a good long while. I like my niceties as much as anyone, but there's something about that pond of poison tar smack dab in the middle of my hometown that leaves me a smidge skeptical about the glories of the free market and the wisdom of the government. And when those two hold hands and get smoochy, you had better watch out.

Fat state subsidies for corporations are not just bad policy. They're bad economics. When corporations and states get too cozy, it brings out the worst in both of them. You get the inefficiency and glacial slowness of bad government mixed with the shortsighted greed of big business on a tear. And this seems to happen whether they cuddle up for right-wing reasons, or ostensibly lefty ones. Under the Reagan-Bush model, you end up with lax regulatory agencies, inordinate subsidies and tax breaks, and a lack of corporate accountability to the community. Under a state-owned Crown corporation like Sydney Steel, you end up with lax regulatory agencies, inordinate subsidies and tax breaks, and a lack of corporate accountability to the community.

If people are going to flap their lips about the glories of the free market, maybe we should try having one first. It would be swell to put a little capitalism back in the capitalism, and a little governance back in the government. The entitlements that corporations enjoy are not merely unfair. They're also antithetical to competition, which is supposedly one of the engines that drives our glorious economy. This lack of competition leads to a lack of choice as well. Not a lack of choice between products;

nope, there are plenty of those. Why, you could pick and choose from thousands of just one product—like a computer, say. But the odds are pretty good that whatever computer you buy, it's going to be running Windows, and the chips inside will come from one of the couple of companies that dominate the industry. No matter what we buy, all our money pretty much ends up in the same few places. The wrappers and the ads are different, but the same few folks, artificial and real, pick up the bucks. Most sectors today are dominated by a few colluding concerns, which hardly squares with classical economic notions like transparency, competition, and free trade.

The global marketplace is riddled with de facto monopolies and oligarchies, neither of which Adam Smith was down with back in the day. When Smith was writing about businesses, he meant something more like a small business, so that the owner's interests were bound up with the quality of the product. Today's free market bears little resemblance to Smith's version of the market: instead of running itself via Invisible Hand, our markets are inextricably entwined with the world's governments, propped up on a cushion of subsidies and reclining on lax laws.

It is clear that corporations excel at churning up a profit. What is unclear is exactly how much we all pay so that they may do so, and what we get out of it. When those profits are skimmed off the top and handed out to CEOs and major shareholders, they aren't shared with mutual fund and pension plan investors, or plowed back into the continued health of the company or into the care and feeding of its workers or into the management of wastes the company produces or into the quality of its products and services. The past twenty years demonstrate that corporations will not invest in such long-term interests, let alone serve the public good, unless they are made to do so, either by law or by force of consumer, share-holder, and employee ire. Corporations evade taxes, cook their books, create big toxic messes, and screw their workers for the best possible reasons: because they can; because it pays; because we, the chumps, are willing to pay for it so long as we get our little sliver of the tasty pie.

The Bush administration has another term to keep on out-Reaganing Reagan, slashing taxes on the rich, spending billions on defense, and racking up record-breaking deficits. After the 2000 debacle, a friend pointed out the limited upside of the election of a fresh batch of familiar Republicans: at least music would get better. He rhymed off lists of great Reagan/Thatcher-era singles, angry desperate rawk and melancholy pop fueled by the general sense of economic and social malaise, like old REM and the Clash, the kind of stuff you hear at a bar on Retro Night. And it started to make sense; Reagan begetting Bush begetting Bush, *Dynasty* sequins and Sid Vicious belts on the runways, the new sad punks, the same old shite. We are living in the undead eighties, all the more powerful for coming back from the dead, like Jesus and zombies. Culture wars, a new evil empire, that Jennifer Lopez video that is *Flashdance*—it's the eighties all over again, even though they only just happened. Now that Dubya is back for four more years, one Retro Night track strikes me as especially apropos: a song by the marvelously mopey Smiths from their 1987 release, *Strangeways, Here We Come,* a bitter little ditty called "Stop Me If You Think You've Heard This One Before."

CHAPTER FIVE

DON'T WORRY ABOUT THE GOVERNMENT

or We Don't Need No Stinkin' Rules

Government does not solve problems; it subsidizes them.

—RONALD REAGAN

Politicians are synonymous with bullshit. It is a truth universally acknowledged that prevarication is practically part of the job description. The last three American presidents have all bullshitted flagrantly and publicly in their own special ways. Reagan thought facts were stupid things, and conjured chimerical scenarios involving wealthy, Caddy-driving welfare queens and air-polluting trees. Bush the elder was more of an omitter, erecting a wall of sentence fragments between his office and his creepy business concerns. Clinton lied about sex and then lied about lying about sex and then dropped bombs on Baghdad during his fib-filled, fib-fueled impeachment. It should be pretty clear by this point in my little screed that I think the current president is a world-historical bullshitter, as his no-bullshit pose—nuance is for pussies!—only makes his bullshit all the bullshittier.

Politicians are among the first people to tell you that politicians are full of shit, decrying their fellows as flip-floppers or

flimflam artists or outright liars. It's no surprise that mud-
slinging is de rigueur on the campaign trail, and has been,
since North America was colonized. Negative campaigning is
not a recent invention. But over the past twenty-five years
political campaigns have gone beyond simply saying that the
other guy is Beelzebub. Now government itself, and in general,
is bad. Nobody seems more delighted to describe, in exquisite
detail, just how corrupt government is than someone who
happens to be running for it, or an elected member of it.

For your consideration: "We propose not just to change its
policies, but even more important, to restore the bonds of
trust between the people and their elected representatives.
That is why, in this era of official evasion and posturing, we
offer instead a detailed agenda for national renewal, a written
commitment with no fine print." Splendid! I could use a government with less cumbersome fine print! "Official evasion
and posturing"—that fairly rolls off the tongue, doesn't it?
Testify, soul brother. What young firebrand could have penned
this feisty manifesto? I regret to inform you, dear reader, that
this stirring invective comes from the preamble to the Contract with America, one of the epic ballads of the ongoing and
oxymoronic conservative or Republican revolution.

Ronaldus Magnus, as some conservatives call him, began
the popular chorus against government strangleholds on free
enterprise. He didn't come up with it, but he spread the notion
that markets do just about everything better than the sucky
old public sector. For the freshman Republican Congress of
1994, this kind of anti-government governance was the object
of revolutionary fervor. Ten years later, Bush's reelection, and
Republican majorities in the House and the Senate, seem to
indicate that the Republican revolution has been a riproaring
success, and that the people want a government that wants less

of itself—at least in word, if not always in deed. Even though
Bush's policies have generated a very big and costly government, including a whole new department, he talked about his
tax cuts in terms of getting government off the backs of the
people, and letting the just plain folks have their own money
and power. He is using the same sort of sell to push privatizing
Social Security. The "ownership society" and "culture of responsibility" are squishy revamps of the language of the Contract.

The Contract was the usual mishmash of deregulation, privatization, and freewheeling free marketeering. But it was
wrapped in a rich, creamy coating of rhetoric about personal
and fiscal responsibility and government accountability. It
called for an audit of the Congress itself for waste, fraud, and
abuse. And though Market Good, Government Bad was the
first psalm in the book of the conservative revolution, it
should be noted that this sort of full-on froth-at-the-mouth
was by no means a solely right-wing phenomenon in the
nineties. Newt Gingrich wouldn't have gotten the kind of press
that he did, including *Time*'s 1995 Man of the Year cover, had
he not glommed on to an anti-government sentiment swirling
about the Zeitgeist. Government-hating transcended party
lines. You had a spectrum of loathing that stretched from the
extreme survivalist build-me-a-compound right all the way to
the latest wave of black-clad bohemian malcontents. It was
Clinton, representing the long-standing official party of great
big government, who declared that "the era of big government
is over."

If you go back to the Founding Fathers, an approach advo-
cated by no less august an historian than Mr. Gingrich himself,
you will find an anti-government streak in American democracy right from the get-go. Jefferson, for example, thought the

best government was the least government. Thomas Paine's classic pamphlet *Common Sense* argues that an independent government is simply a necessary evil; it's either the republic or more British tyranny. Paine certainly isn't chuffed about government in general. He begins his treatise by differentiating between society and government. Society is the realm of voluntary fellow-feeling, but we need government as well, he argues, to punish the inevitable wickedness that threatens the friendly bonds of social life. If we were all sufficiently endowed with conscience, government would be unnecessary. Alas, we are not, and consequently we must enter a social contract, agreeing to surrender up part of our property to furnish the means of protecting the rest. Paine thought it nonsensical that Americans be subject to some distant, tyrannical king, and instead proclaimed that people should live under the rule of law.

I mention Paine at length because I dig him, but also because of the persistence of the phrase "common sense" in conservative policy agendas. The Harris Conservatives in Ontario called their movement the Common Sense Revolution. One of the provisions in the Contract with America was called the Common Sense Legal Standards Reform Act, which called for "reform of product liability laws to stem the endless tide of litigation." Not exactly stick it to the king, but tort reform was the sort of thing that passed for a commonsensical notion in governance at the time. And please understand that by "reform," Newt and company meant "get rid of." If the first psalm in the book of the conservative revolution was Market Good, Government Bad, the second was, We Don't Need No Stinkin' Rules. The freshman Republicans in Congress were hell-bent on doing away with as many ridiculous regulations as possible, thus allowing trade to grow and thrive. They saw themselves as the rightful heirs to Reagan, but this wasn't just morning in

America; this was a revolution, and you were in or out. Congressmen like Newt Gingrich, Dick Armey, and Tom DeLay aggressively led the charge to replace the old Liberal Welfare State with the brand-spankin'-new Conservative Opportunity Society. And if they had to totally shut down the government to save the government, as they did in the 1995 budget dispute, so be it.

In March 1995, that latter-day radical Tom, Tom DeLay, struck a pose next to a five-foot replica of the Statue of Liberty swathed in red tape, and began hacking and slashing away at the hated symbol of old-school bureaucracy. When I was rooting around for exemplary Republicans, and began looking at DeLay, the current House Majority Leader and former House Majority Whip, I liked him for a number of reasons. First, he did fun things like cover statues with red tape. Second, he wasn't as played out and ubiquitous as the Newt. Third, he, and all the lesser Tom DeLays, who share his Christ-and-Mammon creed but lack his diabolical skills, are living proof that I am not paranoid. My most tinfoil-hatted fantasies pale in comparison to the things right-wing radicals like DeLay and his ilk actually say and do. Fourth, and most significant, DeLay is one of the crucial players in the melding of moneyed interests and government.

It would be an understatement to DeClare that DeLay is DeVoted to DeRegulation; "Mr. DeReg" is but one of his nicknames. He is also known as "The Hammer," "The Congressman from Enron," and "The Exterminator." He was known as "Hot-Tub Tom" when he was a multiple martini man, but he has since switched, like Bush, to chugging the Lord. DeLay got the moniker "The Hammer" not for his balloony harem pants or his funny sideways dancing, but for his full-frontal fundraising and no-nonsense way of dealing with Washington's legion of lobbyists. "The Congressman from Enron" is because Enron gave DeLay some dough. And, though I hate to imply anything so salacious as a simple cash-for-favors quid pro quo, DeLay did seem awfully enthused about exempting Enron from energy trading regulations. "The Exterminator" refers to his career previous to politics. DeLay operated a pest-control business in Sugar Land, Texas, and it was there that he saw the way and the truth and the light. Fire ants were eating Texas, and yet the EPA banned the most effective fire ant–slaughtering agent available to the mass bug murderer at the time, on account of them reckoning it was carcinogenic. Nor could he abide the worker safety laws that required fumigators to wear hardhats during routine termite routs. DeLay swore vengence on the bean counters down in Washington for stifling the spirit of free enterprise, and went into politics, a Capra-corny conservative conversion tale indeed.

Since entering politics, DeLay has been the point man for the We Don't Need No Stinkin' Rules movement. He has described the EPA as "the Gestapo of government," and tried to cut its funding. He also wanted to repeal the Clean Air Act. When a reporter asked him if there were any regulatory measures worth keeping, DeLay replied, "Not that I can think of." And just so you know that he is keeping the no-rules thing real down home, the district surrounding Sugar Land boasts a Monsanto plant, a BASF chemical plant, an EPA Superfund mercury site, one of the bigger Dow complexes, and air and water quality that are typically Texan in their terribleness.

Remember that incident in Texas in 2003, when all the Democrats fled to neighboring states to block a redistricting vote that would hand the Republicans more seats? That gerrymandering would be more fine DeLay handiwork. He then used his sway within the federal government to interfere in the protest against the gerrymander, contacting the Federal Aviation Administration to track down those wayward Democrats. This last bit of strong-arming is the substance of one of the ethics complaints filed against DeLay in 2004. The other ethics complaints involve DeLay attempting to influence a colleague in a House vote, and his use of inappropriate corporate contributions to fund Republican campaigns through his political action committee. DeLay's associates are under investigation by a Texas grand jury for the latter transgression as well, and three have already been charged with violating campaign finance law.

Republicans spent the weeks before Christmas vacillating about changing their ethics rules to accommodate the possibility of a DeLay indictment. In January of 2005, the Republicans decided that it would be perfectly fine to strike down a rule that might interfere with DeLay's position as House Majority Leader, should he be charged in Texas. A few days later, however, they reversed this decision. Given that the ethics rules in question were penned by the revolutionary Republican congress of 1994 in the first place, this vote looked very bad. In fact, it looked so bad that even DeLay thought that his colleagues should reverse their decision. However, at the same time, the Republicans also made another change that effectively scuttles future ethics complaints against DeLay or any other offending congress-critters. The ethics committee will no longer launch investigations if it reaches a tie vote on the complaints. The ethics committee is half Republican, half Democrat. Consequently, members of the committee will have to vote against their own parties to launch investigations, which they are often unwilling or unable to do. The outgoing chair of the Ethics Committee, Representative Joel Hefley, is a notable exception to this rule. Even though he is a Republican, he has been fairly zealous in following up on a variety of complaints against DeLay. Of course, this zeal is one of the reasons why he is the *outgoing* chair of the Ethics Committee. It is rumored that his replacement will be a more obedient and obliging Republican, perhaps a DeLay-friendly fellow Texan.

But I'm getting ahead of myself. Let's go back to DeLay denuding Lady Liberty of that red tape, back in 1995. DeLay did not wield the shears of freedom all by his lonesome. Beside him was the chair of Project Relief, lobbyist Bruce Gates, who had helped drum up support for their most recent victory: a moratorium on government health and safety regulations, which passed the house by a vote of 276 to 146. There had been some four thousand rules in the pipeline, leftovers from the Democrats, and the Republicans wanted to head them off at the pass, or at least stall them until they could pass more comprehensive antiregulatory legislation. When *The Washington Post* inquired as to the propriety of numerous industry lobbyists sitting down in DeLay's office to draft provisions of the moratorium bill, DeLay maintained that industry had the expertise. Various members of Project Relief, a super-lobby of 350 industry and corporate concerns, dropped by to make sure that their interests would be served by the bill; for example, UPS wanted to make sure that emissions regulations wouldn't call for a retooling of their fleet of trucks, and Union Carbide was sweating the possibility of facing more fines for failure to report off-duty worker injuries. Once everyone passed the legislation around, and penned a line or two, like some bizarre rich-guy version of that Surrealist party game, Exquisite Corpse, the nice people at Project Relief let loose the lobbying hounds, convincing various Democrats with industries in their districts to come along on the cool new no-rules ride.

A similar bill, floated in the Senate by Bob Dole, enjoyed the favor and the legwork of a like-minded organization of larger manufacturing concerns, the Alliance for Reasonable Regulation. By "reasonable," the car makers and chemical companies meant "less," just as the manufacturers and couriers that made up Project Relief intended to relieve themselves of the burden of excessive regulation. It makes good sense, really. Why go to all the fuss and bother of "bidding defiance to the laws of the nation," as per Jefferson's allegations against moneyed corporations, when it is ever so much easier to simply sashay up to the Hill and have those puppies rewritten?

This sort of folderol bore little resemblance to the legislative process as I remembered it from that *Schoolhouse Rock* song, "I'm Just a Bill." The humble singing scrap of paper that made it all the way to Capitol Hill started very differently: The folks wanted a law and called their congressman, who wrote the law. That seems so desperately mid-seventies, as earnest and outmoded as Jimmy Carter or a macramé plant holder.

DeLay, uncoincidentally, was the second leading fund-raiser for the freshman Republicans in Congress in 1994, bested only by the Newt. He reportedly kept a ledger in his office detailing which lobbies were friendly and unfriendly, based on the amount that their political action committees had given to the Republican machine. DeLay told groups with Democratic ties that they wouldn't see jack until they hired a Republican lobbyist, because he didn't want to deal with "people who wanted to kill the revolution." Okay, whatever you say, Che. This crackdown is sometimes called The K Street Project. And you'll never guess what little Randy DeLay, Tom's bro, became when he grew up: a lobbyist, and a mighty successful one, particularly when lobbying his brother, which he did on behalf of a Mexican cement company and a ginormous railroad merger. Yes, all the brothers going to rise up, come the revolution.

When bipartisan campaign finance legislation became all the rage on Capitol Hill, Mr. DeReg didn't hesitate to poo on the killjoy rule talk. Money wasn't the problem, said DeLay; in fact, money was the very lifeblood of the political system. And Newt, even though he crumbled and shook hands with Slick Willie over the promise of a campaign finance reform bill, maintained that all the player-hating analysis was nothing more than a loony expression of socialist disapproval of the free enterprise system. If a stomach-pill manufacturer could pay 100 million dollars to get a message out, quoth the Newt, why shouldn't we spend that a couple of times over on promoting and producing the political process?

It is understandable that persons like Gingrich and DeLay, who are so wholeheartedly devoted to the pursuit of funds, would consider them the alpha and omega of political life. When the first, much-ballyhooed campaign finance bill choked, it was on account of nobody wanting to be the first to give up all the sweet, sweet donations. It was like a Mexican stand-off, everyone having unwittingly spent themselves into a state of Mutually Assured Donation. Republicans decried contributions from staunchly Democratic unions: Their dues were extortion, plain and simple, pimped out of blue-collar just folks and funneled to pesky liberal do-gooders, regardless of the political preferences of individual workers. Democrats, meanwhile, decried corporate contributions, but largely because the Republicans were better at soliciting them—and they did not express their disapproval by refusing huge corporate contributions to their own campaigns. Oftentimes, big donors bet on both nags: Enron, for example, skewed Republican in keeping with its Texan roots, but threw an unholy heap of cash at the Democrats as well. I think those rich dudes might be on to something. Maybe next election, I'll vote for both guys, too. Whichever way the shit goes down, my ass will be covered.

I don't know if money is, as DeLay claims, the lifeblood of politics. Maybe he needs to act that metaphor out for me again, like he did with that red tape thing: He could inject a Statue of Liberty with a big syringeful of green ink, to represent the healing effects of cash transfusions on the body politic. I'm not a doctor, but if I had to diagnose the American body politic, I do not think I would write "monetary anemia" or "insufficient fundingitis" on its chart.

How about calling money the *food* of politics, as in, "If money be the food of politics, feed on!" The food metaphor works on other levels, too: The body politic can be said to be bulimic. Look at the way voters binge and purge over election cycles, trading Great Society–style liberal largesse for conservatives' cutbacks and capitalism. Gingrich and company claimed that they wanted the government to go on a diet, but at the same time they were fattening their own party coffers. Binge on contributions; purge the regulations. In with the money, out with the governance. Perhaps DeLay could do a press conference in which he appears before a fridge at midnight, eats a giant cake shaped like the Statue of Liberty, and then throws up an omnibus bill outlawing laws against laws that stop the spread of laws. One of his pals from Project Relief could hold his hair back.

Project Relief and the Association for Reasonable Regulation were megalobbies, which is to say, lobbies made up of other lobbies. It is hard to estimate exactly how many active lobbies there are in Washington. In 2002, there were more than twenty-four thousand registered lobbyists there, about forty-five for every member of Congress, a ratio that fairly wallops Surf City's promise of two girls for every boy. Moreover, these estimates merely account for those involved in lobbying at the federal level. There are also thousands of lobbyists pitching woo at the state level, too. Add up all the dough that flows from both levels, and we are talking about at least a billion dollars, maybe even two billion. I leave it to your discretion, Gentle Reader, to judge whether or not the titans of industry would sink that kind of cash into a process that granted them few tangible gains. For example, the most lobby-mobbed issue of the last few years is tax policy. Is it mere happenstance that corporate tax revenues are at historic lows, or is it some damn fine work on the part of influence peddlers?

Of course, lobbying is only one part of the contemporary political equation. Sure, you can pay a lobbyist to get your message out, but you can also just let the sweet, sweet money speak for itself, in the form of campaign contributions. One of the reasons why campaign finance legislation has been a hot topic for the past few years is that the past three U.S elections have been the most expensive ever, until the next one came along. An amended version of McCain's campaign finance bill, the Bipartisan Campaign Reform Act (BCRA), was finally passed in March of 2002, in time for the 2004 election, but it didn't end up curbing campaign contributions or spending. It merely rerouted the copious cataracts of cash into different kinds of slush funds.

To understand how this came to pass, a wee history of U.S. campaign finance law might come in handy. The Federal Election Commission rules were written in 1971, and rewritten throughout the seventies, after the Watergate scandal revealed little tidbits like the fact that Nixon got millions of profoundly illegal clams for the 1972 campaign. The 1974 amendments set contribution limits: An individual could give $1,000 to a candidate, and a political action committee could give $5,000. Total individual donations to the party, political action committees, and specific candidates could not exceed $25,000 per year.

The 1976 Supreme Court decision in a case called *Buckley vs. Valeo* altered these regulations somewhat, challenging the constitutionality of the 1974 changes to the Federal Elections Campaign Act (FECA) on the grounds that the rules infringed on the First Amendment right to free speech. The argument was simply that no significant political expression could take place without spending some money. The Court consequently struck down limits on candidate expenditures, family contributions, and self-contributions, paving the way for eccentric billionaire campaigns à la Steve Forbes and Ross Perot. It also ruled that there could be no limits on the expenditures of candidates and their committees, except in the case of presidential candidates who accepted federal matching funds. But the court upheld the FECA with respect to contribution limits, the disclosure process, and provision of federal funds for presidential elections. Justice Warren Burger issued a partial dissent/partial concurrence in keeping with the partial decision, noting that it was paradoxical of the Justices to limit contributions while permitting theoretically unlimited expenditures. He wrote, "The Act as cut back by the Court thus places an intolerable pressure on the distinction between 'authorized' and 'unauthorized' expenditures on behalf of a candidate; even those with the most sanguine hopes for the Act might well concede the distinction cannot be maintained." Throughout the late seventies, legislators messed with the FECA, trying to retain such distinctions, but by 1979 they further amended it to okay unlimited spending on the part of state and local parties for promotional, get-out-the-vote-type campaign materials, also known as "soft money."

Hard money pays for campaign ads that explicitly declare, "Vote for John Q. Public." Soft money pays for campaign activities that do not use words like "vote" or "elect." Hard money is regulated by the Federal Election Commission (FEC). Soft money is not. The beauty and utility of this bumper-sticker-fund provision didn't dawn on fund-raisers until the late eighties, during the Dukakis campaign. By 1992, both parties had raised about $46.5 million in soft money, versus $219 million of the hard kind subject to FEC regulations. During the 1996 race, soft money tripled, swelling to $150 million, and hard money just about doubled, to $393 million. In the 2000 race, the Republicans raised $466 million in hard money and $250 million in soft money. The Democrats pulled in $275 million in hard money and $245 million in soft money. Throughout 2001 and 2002, Repubs and Dems socked away another $250 million and $246 million, respectively, stashing their soft cash before the November 2002 deadline set by the BCRA.

The BCRA is not as stringent as the first McCain-Feingold bill, which Jesse Helms and the gang filibustered to death. Soft money is out, but in exchange, limits for hard-money contributions have been raised. Even though the BCRA was a compromise bill, it got tied up in court challenges as soon as it passed. The eighty or so court cases challenging the BCRA were collected under the case name of *McConnell vs. FEC*. The McConnell in question is Republican senator Mitch McConnell, one of campaign finance reform's most ardent opponents. He was instrumental in fighting McCain-Feingold, and swore that he would do in the courts what he could not do in the Senate. Republicans seem to adore appealing to the judiciary in this way, their anti-lawsuit rhetoric notwithstanding. McConnell claimed that the BCRA is flat-out unconstitutional, as it contravenes the First Amendment. On December 10, 2004, the Supreme Court decided in favor of the FEC, upholding all the major provisions of the BCRA.

The BCRA was supposed to set stricter guidelines for campaign contributions and check the tide of soft money. But once the soft-money loophole closed, another campaign-financing entity emerged to keep the sweet, sweet funds flowing. The 2004 election marked the rise of the 527, so named for a section of the tax code. The 527s are tax-exempt fundraising organizations, and they disclose their activities to the IRS, not the FEC. This means they are unregulated by the FEC, which makes them look an awful lot like—you guessed it, chum—soft money. The 527s are subject to some BCRA provisions, like the ones that determine when political ads can be aired, but other than that, they are free to deploy their unlimited contributions as they see fit. When fund-raising was split into hard and soft money, there were two kinds of ads. Hard-money ads were allowed to engage in express advocacy. Soft-money ads could only implicitly advocate for a candidate. Soft-money ads were, for the most part, issue ads, or negative speculation about opposing candidates. The 527 ads in the most recent election cycle went beyond these old categories of express and implicit advocacy, into new realms of hyperbole and character assassination. Consider the 527 organization that got the most political bang for its millions: The Swift Vets and POWs for Truth. These vets didn't say a thing about Kerry's policies, or his voting record. Instead, they engaged in innuendo, insinuating that Kerry was a sham war hero, who didn't really deserve his Purple Hearts. Republicans had the unmitigated gall to question Kerry's service record, even though their own candidate couldn't be bothered to show up for all of his draft-deferring National Guard service. This strategy was totally in keeping with the gospel according to Karl Rove: attack your opponent on his strengths, not his weaknesses.

There were, of course, also pro-Kerry 527s, like MoveOn and America Coming Together, which benefited from the largesse of anti-Bush philanthropists like George Soros. These organizations were also very good at soliciting small contributions, particularly over the Internet. In the run-up to the presidential election, pro-Democrat 527s were actually raising and spending more money than the Republican ones. The Republican 527s made a big push in the last three weeks of campaigning, and outspent the Democrats during the final crunch, particularly in battleground states like Ohio. The Progress for America Voter Fund, a consortium of Bush-friendly corporations and muckety-mucks, blew more than $16 million on advertising in the last three weeks of the campaign. Over the course of the 2003–04 campaign cycle, 527s raised and spent more than half a billion dollars. The fundraising totals for 2004 alone were $434 million. These figures are comparable to the figures for soft money before the ban, which indicates that there is just as much money spilling into the electioneering process as there was before, and that the BCRA has merely rerouted the flow.

Fans of campaign financing free-for-alls, like McConnell, often claim that spending helps get out the vote, an issue of the utmost importance in a democracy that is lucky when half its eligible population makes it to the polls. And I actually agree with Senator James Buckley and Eugene McCarthy's argument that forms of political expression depend on spending some bucks. The problem is that this introduces a little something Supreme Court types would call "invidious equality," a situation that is theoretically equal but practically discriminatory. Everyone is protected by the First Amendment. But the First Amendment plus a couple of million bucks can get you the presidential candidate of your choice and maybe even the chance to help pen the laws of the land. Take away the millions and you have the inalienable right to bore people on public transit.

For all the American brag and puff about the 60 percent voter turnout in the 2004 election, the U.S. and Canada have far lower voter turnout rates than most European democracies. (Iceland, with an average voter turnout of 88 percent, is the gold medalist.) And one of the reasons is the perception that it really doesn't matter. To give Ralph Nader his due, special interests *are* running the political process, and they come in two different flavors, which gives everyone something to bitch about. You can write off the government because they're a bunch of do-gooders wasting tax dollars on the quaint old New Deal, or you can shrug and give up because they are a wholly owned corporate subsidiary. Either way, it's out of your hands and way over your head. While the 60 percent voter turnout in the 2004 election is a marked improvement over the 50 percent that dragged themselves to the polls in 2000, one group of potential voters remained resolutely apathetic in 2004, despite the best efforts of crusading celebs like P. Diddy. Young people are still avoiding the polls like the plague, even though it is the young who will bear the costs of the current regime's fiscal irresponsibility.

In Canada, we enjoy some semblance of a social safety net, and our political rhetoric is not as polarized or fervent as the speeches of the Republican revolutionaries, or their Democratic detractors. One reason our politics are not so polarized is that we spend far less time electioneering in Canada. The United States has more elections than Canada, and longer, louder campaigns for those elections. Though Canada may be more moderate than its neighbor to the south, we too suffer from modern political malaises such as voter apathy, influence peddling, and corruption. Our politicians don't get caught at hotels with their mistresses; they give their cronies money to build hotels. The reigning Liberals also like to blow millions on well-intentioned boondoggles like the national gun registry or the sponsorship scandal, an ongoing imbroglio that has revealed the transfer of beaucoup de federal bucks to shady Quebec ad agencies for the ostensible promotion of Canadian identity. Moreover, lest you mistake the Great White North for a worker's paradise, our current prime minister, Paul Martin, is a junior, just like Bush. Paul Martin Sr. never made it all the way to the highest office in the land, but he was a career politician who raised a career politician. Paul Martin Jr. is also très riche. He signed his shipping company, Canada Steamship Lines, over to his sons when he took office, to avoid conflict of interest allegations, but the company has a long history of taking advantage of offshore tax breaks to boost its revenues. In fact, when Paul Martin was finance minister, he passed a law against offshore tax havens and then promptly moved his operations from Liberia to Barbados. Liberia was subject to the new law. Barbados was not. This is simply to say that even in the seemingly tax-friendly confines of Soviet Canuckistan, the politician responsible for collecting and spending our tax dollars has dodged millions in taxes himself.

Mr. DeReg and the Newt are quick to claim that money is the lifeblood of the political process, but the radical Republicans were never quite revolutionary enough to suggest a fiscal equivalent to the universal suffrage that makes democracy democratic. If money is the lifeblood of politics, then what's voting? The lymph? Or is it the bile? The last couple of presidents have gotten about half the popular vote, but the popular vote has been about half of the eligible people, which is not even to mention the hordes that are not eligible or registered. The dictionary definition of democracy is government by the majority of the people, not one quarter of them. Maybe we need a new word. There's a whole buffet of little-used-cracies we could retrieve from their relative obscurity; you've got your plutocracy, sure, but then there's gerontocracy (government by the old), or my personal fave, kakistocracy (government by the worst citizens).

Spending billions to elect politicians we are none too thrilled about gives the whole process an air of ceremonial futility, the same sense one gets when one is sitting through a very expensive wedding ceremony celebrating a marriage with decidedly mediocre prospects. The place looks great, they spared no expense, but this public-elected-officials match is only going to last a couple of years, tops, and then it'll all end in tears, dear. (Gee, I wonder who will get to keep all the loot?) The purpose of government, for people like Paine, was to serve as a check on bad behavior and a guarantor of liberty, not to get all pally with you. This is why government is not inherently swell, and should be kept as small as possible. The state should be big enough to protect the rights and freedoms of individuals, but not so big that it infringes upon them. But the current avatars of smaller government, Republican and Democrat alike, have somehow magicked up a state that is Jabba-like in its girth, increasingly disinclined to protect and represent the citizenry via regulation, and increasingly inclined to diddle with your personal freedom in countless asinine ways, like throwing your ass in the pokey for possession of a dime bag.

The notion that Republicans are the party of fiscal responsibility, as opposed to those tax-and-spend liberal Democrats, is laughable, after massive deficits under Reagan and titanic ones under Bush. If you think this is just a result of bad financial luck, then you aren't hip to the Grover Norquist master plan, which has been kicking around the Capitol for years: Get government so small, so broke, that you can drown it in a bathtub. Spend and slash until there is no government! But for all their anti-government rhetoric, the Republicans are people who have been hanging around the White House for decades, like Dick Cheney and Donald Rumsfeld. It's not too hard to dig up pictures of the boys with their muttonchop sideburns, wide collars, and big fat ties, from way back in the Nixon era. And even the ones who aren't fossils from previous regimes, like the members of the Republican freshman class, clearly love the great game of politics, even if they hate the government that allows them to practice politics, the government that they, um, are.

Government will never be fun and cool so long as it's a bunch of old white guys arguing about math and making rules. Rules are no fun. It may shock and amaze you to discover that I am no more in favor of idiot regulations than Tom DeLay is. Part of the problem with government regulations is that there are so many, it is impossible to enforce the ones that matter, and they are written in a legalese that fairly defies consciousness. Just try to read the North American Free Trade Agreement—I double-dare you to get through even twenty pages. Yet that unreadable document is currently changing your life. If we are going to dumb this system down, I say we dumb it all the way, with really stupid rules that say what they mean and mean what they say, like the You're Never Going to Spend All of That Act or the Hey, Clean Up After Yourself Bill.

The fact that both the presidential candidates in the 2000 and 2004 elections were to the manor born was the last little funny "I knew Thomas Paine and you, sir, are no Thomas Paine" thing. Why stick it to the king when you can thrall to the charms of your new family dynasties? People keep invoking common sense in their stump speeches, but government hasn't exhibited much of either lately. It is my fondest hope that something will put the demos back in democracy. But I fear that I may someday have to explain to my progeny that Jenna and Barbara, the first female candidates for president, are in fact the scions of a political empire that stretches back at least three generations. And that we used to have these things called debates before President Schwarzenegger decided Jell-O wrestling was a better way to test the candidates' mettle. Perhaps the Gipper was on to something: Government doesn't solve problems like George Bush, Dick Cheney, and Tom DeLay. It merely subsidizes them.

CHAPTER SIX

PILLZAPOPPIN'!

The Rise of Big Pharma

Paxil . . . Your Life Is Waiting.

—Ad for Paxil

A few short years ago, when American politicians blustered about the tide of drugs coming into the U.S. from Canada, they were talking about marijuana, primarily British Columbian bud. These days, U.S. officials are still making similar statements, but not about the trade in illegal drugs. The new hot-button issue is prescription drugs. In 2003 alone, according to estimates from the U.S. Department of Health and Human Services, Americans spent $700 million dollars buying Canadian prescription drugs. The Food and Drug Administration and the Department of Health and Human Services insist that Canadian drugs, particularly those ferried from online pharmacies, may be unsafe, and have issued numerous letters and warnings about skeevy northern merch. Nevertheless, some state governments, such as Rhode Island and Vermont, have challenged the FDA and demanded the right to buy cheaper Canadian drugs. As supporters of the initiative point out, Canada has its own perfectly lovely FDA, and our regulatory agency is *not* funded by industry user fees. America's is, and has been, since 1992.

The importation controversy is only the most recent example of a growing concern about the price of prescription drugs. In December of 2003, Bush signed the Medicare Modernization Act, which includes a prescription drug benefit to try to help defray the rising costs of prescription drugs. The benefit will cost about 593 billion dollars, according to the Congressional Budget Office. While it is certainly salutary that the government is doing something about those poor old grandmas who have to choose between food and pills, the proposed benefit does not address more fundamental problems with the pharmaceutical industry. The reason Canadian drugs are cheaper than U.S. ones is that Canada, like most industrialized nations, exerts modest price controls over brand-name prescription drugs. In the U.S., price controls are dismissed as commie-talk and a threat to innovation. The prescription drug benefit doesn't even propose modest cost reductions, like bulk buying of pharmaceuticals at reduced costs. Rather, the plan simply injects more cash into Medicare-funded private drug benefit schemes, making it just as much of a benefit and a boon for the pharmaceutical and insurance industries as it is for people in need. Picking up part of the tab, swell though that may be, doesn't do a damn thing to combat or censure Big Pharma's really serious trespasses, like profiteering, and selective release of their own research.

It should come as no surprise that pharmaceutical companies are among the world's biggest concerns. What could be an easier sell than drugs? North Americans love themselves some drugs. While it is difficult to put an exact price tag on that love, given the secrecy that shrouds much of the drug market, it is safe to estimate that we spend hundreds of billions of dollars on drugs annually. U.S. prescription drug spending alone reached approximately $200 billion in 2002. Over-the-counter medication accounted for another $17 billion or so that year, but this figure does not account for OTC sales at Wal-Mart, the nation's biggest retailer, so we can add at least another $10 billion to that figure. The Office of National Drug Control Policy reckons that Americans blew about $36 billion on cocaine, $12 billion on heroin, $10 billion on marijuana, $5 billion on amphetamines, and $2 billion on exotic miscellaneous substances like E in the year 2000, the last year for which their stats are available. This pushes our rough estimate into the hundreds of billions, and we have not even reckoned with the alcohol, tobacco, and caffeine industries—the multibillion-dollar legal drug concerns that supply the socially acceptable substances in your lattes and cosmopolitans, and the increasingly verboten nicotine. And then there's the growing field of nutritional supplements and herbal treatments, not to mention the burgeoning trend of "nutraceuticals"—for example, orange juice laced with calcium—and "cosmeceuticals."

Everybody must get stoned! We drug the old. We drug the women, ladling out the mother's little helpers and gross buckets of estrogen. We drug the men, to keep them hard and hairy and stave off their heart attacks. We drug the children: Time for your Ritalin, Timmy! We even drug the beasts of the field, what with a chunk of the multibillion-dollar pet-care industry going to tranks for Fido. We dose our livestock with so many antibiotics and hormones that one could prescribe a course of steak tartare for routine infections and hot flashes. Oh, and then after we take all the pills, we piss them into the water. You might think you're clean and sober, but unless you're Amish or a fundamentalist vegan, you have *something* humming through your bloodstream or stored in your fatty tissues. Call it secondhand pharmacopoeia.

Even these staggering sums fail to account for another couple of billion dollars that represents the most insidious kind of drug spending, the spending that tells us to buy drugs in the first place, and specifies exactly which drugs we should be buying. When I said that we love ourselves *some* drugs, I wasn't just being folksy. As you well know, from having been told ad nauseam in nauseating ads, some drugs are good and other drugs are bad. The drugs that are good are very, very good. The drugs that are bad are horrid.

Let's start with the horrid ones. I have been witness to anti-drug rhetoric for the whole of my short life and vividly remember Nancy's "Just Say No" campaign, and the egg that was your brain frying in the pan that was drugs, and the update in which the girl wrecked her kitchen with the frying pan. That last ad at least acknowledged that drug use will mess up your kitchen—which is demonstrably true. A bout of the munchies can result in sticky surfaces and scattered snack debris, and you can never get all the hot-knife residue off the family silver. Kidding aside, the jackboot-heavy message of each year's new anti-drug ads is that drugs will kill you, and other people, too. So don't do any, ever, kids.

The most recent cycle of anti-drug ads I recall were particularly bullshitty. One features two young dudes hanging around a basement, smoking pot and playing with a gun. One of the boys shoots himself in the head. The joint is supposed to be the bad guy in this ad, but, as many people have pointed out, it works way better as an ad for gun control. There was also a series of ads that linked marijuana to Osama with a rinky-dink, child-narrated "This-is-the-house-that-Jack-built" chain of causation. While some warlords have done a brisk trade in heroin, most marijuana—it being a stinky, heavy thing—comes from locales far closer to home than the Middle East, such as Mexico, Canada, and the decommissioned family farms of Red America.

Such ads are, of course, only salvos in a larger battle I choose to call the War on Some Drugs, an unjust war if ever there was one. During George W. Bush's first term in office, that loon Ashcroft used anti-terrorism laws to collar drug offenders, including Tommy Chong, maker of fine glass pipes. When Tommy Chong, formerly of Cheech and Chong, is getting busted for possession of designer bongcraft, you know that U.S. prosecutions have gotten out of hand. As I'm sure you are aware, prohibition is a price support for black-market cartels and the cause of most drug-related violence. It didn't work with alcohol during Prohibition, and it certainly is not working now. We could save a lot of money on law enforcement and incarceration by treating addiction medically, rather than legally. Hell, we could even make tax dollars from the legalization of the soft Some Drugs, which would be entirely in keeping with the government's role as a purveyor of such ruinous vices as gambling, tobacco, and booze. And you certainly don't need me to tell you that most of the ostensibly bad drugs are more venerable and time-tested than those newfangled Big Pharma drugs that sometimes turn out to have cataclysmic side effects.

There are two main things, beyond the expense and trampling of civil liberties, about the War on Some Drugs that bother me. First, that anti-drug crusaders tend to be hopped up on pills, liquor, God, or their own righteous zeal. My favorite example of this is the infamous 1970 photo of Nixon and Elvis, after the pill-popping president made the pill-gobbling rock god an unofficial deputy in the War on Some Drugs. Second, the War on Some Drugs is largely a war on the poor. The cartels have lawyers and bodyguards and havens to protect themselves from justice. The minor players and users do not. Some drugs are classier than others, but the abjectness of the drug user's condition, and the force of prohibition against them, is dependent on the class of the user, not on the effects of the substance itself. Woe betide the collared crackhead from Any Ghetto, who can look forward to a stint in prison. Would that he, like Noelle Bush or Rush Limbaugh, had the resources for revolving-door rehab.

I have tried several of the Some Drugs, the operative word being *tried*. I drew my line in the sand at hard drugs like crack and H, but I have certainly inhaled—and popped, guzzled, snorted, and swallowed. My life didn't go straight to hell, and I encountered most of these substances, controlled and uncontrolled, in stolid middle-class surroundings. I didn't care much for most of them, but was glad that I had given them a whirl and seen what all the fuss was about. I was never arrested or assaulted or violently ill or driven spontaneously mad. The only drug that has ever made me feel truly wretched is alcohol, the universal solvent of North American good times. I suspect this reflects the drug experience of the vast majority—try a smidge of this and that at a party—but it's the recovering celebs, shattered junkies, brain-dead Phish followers, and ladies who drive home with a body stuck on the front of their cars that you hear about when you hear about drug use. Nobody gives you an honest warning, like that coke may make you an asshole, or that E may cause you to hug total strangers and dance to lousy music.

The only illegal drug I liked, and continue to like, is pot. We have been on the verge of decriminalizing small amounts of marijuana for personal use up here in Soviet Canuckistan for the past couple of years, but have yet to do so. Canada did pass a medical marijuana law in 2001, and set up a contract with a company called Prairie Plant Systems to establish a pot farm in Flin Flon, Manitoba, to provide marijuana for patients who meet the stringent guidelines, and to provide pot for medical research. The January 2005 stats from the Office of Cannabis Medical Access, the agency that administers the program, show that about eight hundred patients are legally allowed to smoke pot, and five hundred patients are allowed to grow a little for their personal use. Critics of the program argue that there isn't sufficient scientific evidence that medical marijuana works. This canard has also been used by U.S. federal drug warriors when meddling with Compassion Clubs in the states that allow medical use of marijuana. While smoking anything does damage the lungs, people have turned to the kind bud for thousands of years to soothe pain, aid sleep, and stimulate the appetite. You cannot overdose on it, unlike many pharmaceuticals. As far as I'm concerned, if it's good enough for Queen Victoria's cramps, then it's fine for you and me, too. It's all well and good to want to keep pot away from the wee developing spuds, but you have to be a merciless puritan to insist we should deny the anodyne charms of a benign weed to the palsied, the cancerous, the seizing, and the wasting away.

Of course, it's not just the puritans who are keeping the ganja down. Big Pharma is also a player. The Partnership for a Drug-Free America, the nonprofit organization that produced some of the anti-drug ads I referred to earlier, is the beneficiary of hundreds of thousands of dollars in donations from tobacco companies, alcohol companies, and the most generous donors of all, pharmaceutical companies. Drug companies contribute about half the money that goes into making Partnership for a Drug-Free America ads. Big Pharma is happy to whip up a batch of Marinol, its own saleable form of THC, but they don't want you frying your sweet little egg of a brain with that amateur shit from the street. They want you to take the good drugs—the patented, prescribed fruits of Big Pharma.

Perhaps the only thing as distasteful as the drugs-are-bad ads are the obliviously chirpy drugs-are-good ones. In keeping with the general ad creep, ads for drugs have increased and spread into more media. Such up-with-pharma ads are a recent innovation. In 1997, the Federal Trade Commission decided to allow more direct-to-consumer (DTC) advertising of prescription drugs, and pharmaceutical companies now spend more than $2.7 billion a year shilling their pills. The only Western nations that permit such advertising are New Zealand and the United States. The Canadian government is trying to decide whether or not to allow DTC ads, but this is an utterly moot point, given that most Canadians watch oodles of American television, and I have seen "ask your doctor" ads run on Canadian television for months without any Health Canada crackdown.

I'll return to the topic of DTC advertising, but first, it is important to note just how big Big Pharma is. Tech, schmech— the savvy investor has known for many moons that pharmaceuticals are the solid bets. A friend of mine made sweet returns on his modest investments throughout the bubble's bust, when everyone else's portfolios were tanking. I never saw him read the financial section. He preferred Baudelaire and haiku. When I asked him what his secret was, he summed it up succinctly: drugs. Ah yes, grasshopper, drugs, the answer to so many questions. Pitted skin? Bad mood? Going bald? Getting limp? Nothing that a little Accutane, Paxil, Rogaine, and Viagra can't fix.

Those are just the lifestyle pills you'll see on television and in magazines. The Valley of the Dolls stretches far deeper and wider than that. There are all the disease-specific pills: the heart and cholesterol pills people pop to fend off the nation's number one killer, cardiovascular disease; and the AIDS cocktails, and varying hellacious regimes of cancer drugs. Then there's the galaxy of painkillers and sleep-inducing elixirs, and all the psychiatric drugs that have yet to achieve the marquee status of Prozac. Then there is the gastrointestinal superstar, Prilosec, an acid-reflux remedy that has spawned a spin-off for the related pain of esophageal erosions, Nexium. And let us not forget the arthritis blockbusters like Celebrex and its re-called fellow, Vioxx, which brings me to another vast pharma-ceutical category: drugs for the ravages of old age. While other cultures venerate their elders and treat them as sages, we excel at keeping our old fogies stoned. Chances are, the most pixi-lated pill-poppin' rave kid is strung out on only half as many chemicals as your average golden-ager. The majority—more than 80 percent—of seniors take prescription drugs. They also take more prescription drugs than younger people. Over 40 percent report using more than three prescription drugs.

The downside of all of these miraculous pills are that they don't come cheap. Health care costs have ballooned all over the industrialized world, and pharmaceutical costs are part of that massive swelling. The United States, the globe's leader in health expenditures, spent about 15 percent of its GDP on health care in 2002, according to the Organization for Eco-nomic Cooperation and Development (OECD). In dollars, that's over $1 trillion, more than double what it was in 1985. Part of this can be blamed on inflation, but a larger share is due to expensive new technologies, the growing needs of an aging population, and the increased price and usage of prescription drugs. The 2004 OECD report notes that costs for prescription drugs grew twice as fast as other health care costs, driving up the overall total.

The Kaiser Foundation did a breakdown of the three factors driving rising drug spending from 1997 to 2002, finding that 42 percent of the increase was due to more drug sales. This is a trend that has been going on for a long time. From 1980 to 2002, prescription drug use tripled. Newer, more expensive brand-name drugs replacing older, more inexpensive ones accounted for another 34 percent of the increase. Price hikes accounted for the other 25 percent. This trinity of increased sales, spiffy new products, and higher prices may be tough on Grandma, but it is fantastic for pharmaceutical companies. From 1995 to 2002, Big Pharma was by far the most profitable sector listed in the Fortune 500. In 2003, they slid to third, behind oil and banking, who had blockbuster years. But big Big Pharma profits are another long trend. The prescription drug industry has enjoyed profit margins two and three times as hefty as those of other industries over the past twenty years. To give you some sense of the gap between Big Pharma and other sectors, consider this: In 2002, which wasn't even the best year of their reign, Big Pharma's profits exceeded the total profits of the other 490 companies on the Fortune 500.

In the early nineties, the industry began to face criticism for the rising cost of drugs from managed care organizations eager to cut their own costs. Big Pharma also has to reckon with a tenacious Gray Power lobby that has all the time in the world to circulate petitions, write angry letters, and call in to talk radio. You can't find a more tear-jerking photograph than a gaggle of frail seniors taking a bus to Canada to fill their prescriptions. It packs a PR wallop. Those poor dear little grannies shouldn't be on that bus! If seniors are on a bus en masse, they should be en route to a leaf tour or to hear Wayne Newton playing Branson, enjoying some golden-years leisure, not scrimping on scrips.

The standard Big Pharma argument against charges of profiteering is that scientific research requires big bucks. Those selective serotonin reuptake inhibitors (SSRIs) aren't made of pixie dust and moonbeams; it takes years of hard work by millions of geeks in white coats, tormenting countless small mammals, peering into microscopes, and penning lengthy studies to find a new drug. According to the nice people at the Pharmaceutical Researchers and Manufacturers of America, it can cost up to $500 million to bring a drug to market, and only a fraction of all drugs developed ever make it. Another industry figure claims it costs $800 million to create a new drug. Whenever hated topics like price controls and patent monopolies come up, Big Pharma pleads science and implies that less money or shorter patents means less science means fewer miracle cures. We need to pay for our research, they say, and protect that research from competitors who might spirit the miraculous new chemicals away.

Here's the rub: Big Pharma doesn't pick up the tab for all the research that creates the miraculous new chemicals. In fact, when you break it down, research money flows from a variety of sources. Much of it is conducted at public facilities that use taxpayer dollars, courtesy of the National Institutes of Health (NIH). Then there are the ones that come from universities. Then there are chemicals developed in other countries that get patented and introduced in the U.S., like Celexa, a leading SSRI originally developed by the Danish firm H. Lundbeck. A report by Ralph Nader's advocacy group, Public

Citizen, contends that fully 85 percent of the research and development behind the top five drugs of 1995 actually came
from taxpayer-funded studies or foreign research.

Tamoxifen, the breast cancer drug, is a nice example. It began
as a British birth control pill in the sixties. The Brits tested it as
a breast cancer treatment throughout the seventies and eighties. Money from the American taxpayer funded tons and tons
of studies and tests in the nineties, and continues to fund research to this day. A billion-dollar concern called AstraZeneca
patented it for sale and pays a wee royalty to the NIH while
making millions and millions. Tamoxifen is the most widely
prescribed breast cancer drug, and they're testing it as a preventative measure for at-risk women, even though some studies show that it may cause strokes or other cancers. People pay
way more for it in the States than in Canada or in Europe, even
though it's the same drug from the same company with plants
all over the globe. And when not making cancer drugs—oh,
genius of capitalism!—AstraZeneca manufactures pesticides.

The Naderites also point to the preponderance of "me-too"
drugs, that is, drugs that are a lot like existing popular drugs.
Until 1992, there was a way of determining whether or not a
drug was truly a revolutionary breakthrough, or simply a vari-
ation on a theme, as Paxil and Zoloft are to Prozac. The Food
and Drug Administration used to classify all new drugs based
on one of three categories. Class A drugs were important therapeutic gains, Class B modest ones, and Class C the copycats
that duplicated existing products. The Bush *père* administration scuttled this classification system at the urging of the
pharmaceutical lobby. The lobbyists were pleased about their
success, and no wonder: Half the drugs approved between
1982 and 1991 were class C, and 31 percent class B. A measly
16 percent made grade A. It's not just the Naderites who are

fuming, either. The former editor of *The New England Journal of Medicine*, Dr. Marcia Angell, argues that two-thirds of the new drugs the FDA approves are mere me-toos. If you're going to brag about the innovation, Big Pharma, how's about you magic up a cancer cure that doesn't make other cancer, instead of making Antidepressant Potion Number Nine or Viagra: The Sequel?

The $500 million per drug figure seems awfully generous, too, when you consider the way research is being conducted by a growing clinical trial industry. In 1999, the *New York Times* ran a couple of deeply creepy investigative reports about cost-cutting and outsourcing in the drug industry. Clinical research has traditionally been the work of academics working under the auspices of universities or teaching hospitals. But academics are not particularly speedy people, and speed is the new watchword in the highly competitive drug-testing market. Consequently, more and more private research companies are conducting clinical trials. Universities have lost about a third of their clinical trials over the past couple of years to other forms of testing. More independent doctors are also performing tests. In 1990, only about four thousand U.S. doctors performed clinical trials for new drugs. By 1997, that number had reached 11,662. Doctors were frequently offered bonuses for signing up enough patients for a trial; one was offered $50,000 if he could round up fourteen guinea pigs for a test of a Merck hypertension drug. Other doctors regularly receive faxes encouraging them to cash in by either running trials or simply recruiting test subjects. The *Times* investigation also found that many of the doctors running tests had little experience doing so, and often ran studies outside their areas of expertise. And wherever and however the research occurs, drug companies ultimately control which results get published and publicized and which ones get buried.

Speed isn't just the watchword for pharmaceutical companies, either. The Food and Drug Administration, which approves all new drugs in the U.S., has picked up its pace. Part of the reason it has picked up the pace is that the industry is paying it to do so. Sick and tired of a balky, underfunded, ponderous drug approval process, industry began paying user fees to get their dope stamped with the federal okay. A 1992 bill called the Pharmaceutical Drug User Fee Act (PDUFA) meant that industry ponied up six-digit fees for every new drug they submitted, in exchange for approval processes that took only six months or a year, rather than two or three years. While the PDUFA has funded more staff at the FDA, and the government hails the program as a success for patients, some critics have argued that the snappier turnaround time for more new drugs may well have something to do with a rise in adverse drug reactions.

Don't misunderstand me: Our prodigious appetite for legal drugs is not entirely misguided. Pills sure do beat a poultice or a good bleeding, and they are less invasive and traumatic than surgery. In fact, it is their very convenience that makes us so dependent on them, and that offers grounds for worry. After all, William S. Burroughs described junkies as the ultimate consumers. They'll pay any price, and they'll wait for the man, so long as they can get their soma. But God only knows what effects any of the current blockbuster drugs will have in twenty-five years, or in the children of people who take them.

Oh, sure, you pay the man and you takes your chances, but maybe it's not the best idea to go swallowing and wallowing in all sorts of relatively new chemicals in a big rush. In the eighties, 233 prescription drugs came to market; in the nineties, that was up to 370, thanks in part to clinical trial and FDA approval times being shortened in the interest of getting drugs to market as quickly as possible. Big Pharma's line is pretty simple: Callooh callay, o frabjous day, more people can get their hands on more medicine. This is the same basic argument you hear from the up-with-the-stock-market types. If more people are doing it, and there is increased participation in the market, it must be good. At the risk of pissing on the progress parade, an increased market share is also an increased radius of consequences. If the markets tank now, more people feel it. If a bad drug somehow makes it to market, more people run the risk of taking it. The most recent example of a drug gone wrong is Vioxx, the arthritis blockbuster that Merck withdrew from the market in fall 2004. Clinical trials found, in the euphemese of the press release, "there was an increased relative risk for confirmed cardiovascular events." If 488,000 Google hits for the phrase "vioxx recall" are any indication, then the class action suit filed against Merck should be a mother. The other big arthritis drugs, such as Celebrex and Bextra, are also being subjected to side-effect scrutiny and the specter of litigation.

The idea that the people have spoken, and have asked for drugs, glosses over the fact that the people are spoken to before they speak. According to a few estimates, those great Big Pharma research budgets are only half as big as the corresponding advertising and marketing budgets. This brings us back to the pharma ads. There have been prescription drug ads running in newspapers and magazines since the early eighties, but it was not until 1997 that the FTC relaxed standards to allow electronic advertising. Since then, ad spending has mushroomed. In 1991, pharmaceutical manufacturers spent about $50 million on "ask your doctor" advertising. In 2001, they spent $2.7 billion. Big Pharma also spent about 12 billion clams in 2000 on marketing to doctors—in the form of samples, paraphernalia, and junkets to exotic places.

There are three main types of DTC ads. The help-seeking ad describes the ailment and suggests you consult a clinician. The reminder ad mentions the company and product. The product claim ad puts the pill and the ill together and lists the benefits of the drug. Most companies rely on all three kinds— an advertising trifecta!—to roll out a new blockbuster. Supporters of DTC advertising claim that it helps increase public awareness about genuinely harmful conditions that often remain undiagnosed and untreated. Big Pharma even goes so far as to take credit for getting people off their duffs and into doctors' offices. The industry insists that DTC ads increase diagnoses of undertreated conditions, improve treatment compliance, destigmatize disease, and inform patients. No longer does all the knowledge and power rest with the doctor, they say: the ads empower consumers to take charge of their health and ask for treatments by name.

Whether or not they're "empowering," a word that sounds especially suspect coming from a marketing department, drug ads are certainly among the odder spots you'll see on TV and in magazines: strange dialogues between marvelous benefits and uncomfortable or potentially lethal side effects. TV ads are also duty-bound to mention a toll-free number, website, or print ad where the consumer can find the full FDA product insert, listing all the contraindications and potential consequences.

The most advertised drugs are remedies for chronic conditions like heartburn, cholesterol, allergies, and depression. A typical spot begins with a disembodied voice oozing concern: "Are you suffering from [random disorder]?" In case you're not up on said disorder, the voice then describes the symptoms, usually an assemblage of banal complaints: no energy, trouble sleeping, various pains. But then the voice warns that these minor hobgoblins may well be a more serious business.

Voilà: the pill. This is followed by some improbable image, like Dorothy Hamill doing a few triple axles at the rink (Vioxx) or a social anxiety disorder sufferer turned smooth operator (Paxil). The very end is a fast, breezy, by-the-way list of all the side effects and contraindications.

The ad for Nexium, the new proton pump inhibitor (PPI) from AstraZeneca, the makers of hit PPI Prilosec, is a good example of the standard script. Pleasant-looking middle-aged folks before a computer-generated backdrop of eroded cliffs urge you to try today's purple pill. Then the voice-over describes the trauma of esophageal erosions—and you thought you had heartburn—and reminds you, again, about today's purple pill. The by-the-way for Nexium is that it may cause abdominal pain, diarrhea, and headaches. This is to say that your heartburn pill may well do nothing more than move your stomachache two inches south, and give you the trots to boot. Oh, and what is Nexium made of? There were two different chemicals in Prilosec. One of them is Nexium. Prilosec is en route to generic cheapness, and so they are trying to sell you half the pill for many times the dough with a new name for your flaming gnaw in the gut. But, hey, ask your doctor! Maybe the little purple pill will allow you to keep on eating at Taco Bell with gay abandon, free of fiery belches, well past your college years. Or maybe the very idea of the purple pill will prove so psychologically powerful that you'll be willing to ignore the fact that the side effects are worse than the malady itself.

The term for the cure that is worse than the ailment is "disease-switching," chemo being the most horrific example. Plenty of people have adjusted to lesser, routine side effects ranging from loss of appetite to loss of libido. But what happens when the side effects of the latest wonder drug seem to include going postal at one's place of employ? Lilly has faced more than two hundred lawsuits with respect to Prozac, many for horrific wrongful deaths, including suicides and murder-suicides. The majority of these suits have been settled out of court, or have failed to draw an arrow from violent behavior to Prozac use. Similar suits have also been filed against the makers of Paxil and Zoloft.

Thus far, the standard Big Pharma defense has been three-fold. First, the FDA approved the drug ages ago, and the FDA don't make no mess, no sir. Second, millions and millions of people take the drug, and only a teeny-tiny percentage of them exhibit these aberrant behaviors. What is the loopiness of one, compared to the salvation of the multitudes? The last line of defense is simply to shift the blame from the cure to the disease. Of course the dude snapped and killed his family—he was depressed, remember? If only we could have given him more drugs, sooner. Still, critics of pharmaceutical manufacturers like to point to the presence of our most popular pills in the medicine chests of the infamously deranged. Police found Prozac capsules in the van belonging to Mark Barton, the Atlanta day trader who killed his family, opened fire at his brokerage, and then committed suicide. Young school-shooter Kip Kinkel was on Prozac, and Eric Harris, one of the Columbine killers, was prescribed Luvox, a Prozac copycat.

The last two examples point to another disturbing trend in prescription drug use, namely, increased drug use by children. In 1998, approximately 500,000 folks under eighteen took one of the leading SSRIs. The number doubled by 2002, in spite of the fact that there was scant scientific literature about the effects of such drugs on children. Some kids even got double-dosed, having been prescribed an SSRI together with the popular juvenile cure-all, Ritalin. In 2004, inspired by a British crackdown on the overprescription of SSRIs for kids and studies that indicated the drugs sometimes caused more frequent thoughts of suicide, the FDA put a black box warning, the most severe, on antidepressants. Antidepressant prescriptions for young people have declined since the suicide studies became headline news.

The FDA has started to look into the effects of adult drugs on the kids who take them and has come up with something called the pediatric exclusivity clause, which allows drug makers to receive six-month extensions on their patents to study the effects of their drugs on children. Since the FDA introduced pediatric exclusivity, approximately three hundred drugs have been submitted for pediatric testing, a dramatic increase over the dozen or so pediatric tests that took place over the previous decade. My big problem with pediatric exclusivity is that the financial incentive may well motivate manufacturers to test drugs on children, regardless of whether or not kids actually need those drugs. For example, tamoxifen has been undergoing pediatric trials. I guess they weren't fooling around about using their product as a preventative measure, if they're giving it to kids who don't even have breasts yet. . . .

If we are going to treat kids with drugs, then it is obvious that we will have to test drugs on kids. But shouldn't that pediatric testing be incorporated into the initial drug review process for drugs kids actually need? Maybe we should see how drugs affect kids before we actually release them to the general public, particularly if thousands of doctors have proven themselves willing to write off-label prescriptions for the under-eighteen set.

Pediatric exclusivity is but one way Big Pharma tries to duck the inevitable day when the patent runs out and lower-priced generics begin to dilute the market. Another way to try to stave it off is to apply for new patents based on slight changes to original formulas, like moving from tablets to caplets, or fiddling with the dosage delivery system. Recent examples of this phenomenon include Paxil CR and Wellbutrin XL, both allegedly longer lasting than their previous incarnations. This hardly seems a significant improvement, however, given that *all* SSRIs take a few days to work their way out of your system. Some pharmaceutical companies stave off the coming of cheap generics by striking sweetheart deals with generic manufacturers, paying them off to delay their product launches. Still others are notorious for filing phony patents on superficial aspects of the pill, or specific parts of the active ingredient, to delay the inevitable. Patent infringement lawsuits against generic makers, which can delay the launch of a generic for up to thirty months, or for the length of the court case, are par for the course. Even an extra six months without competition can add up to hundreds of millions.

There's a world of global patent debates raging beyond all this domestic intellectual property chicanery. Both the World Trade Organization and the United Nations have been addressed by many activists arguing that epidemics in poor countries justify the emergency production of mass quantities of cheap generics. An Indian company, Cipla, was ready to prepare a retroviral cocktail for Doctors Without Borders to distribute in Uganda and Ghana, when GlaxoSmithKline got all shirty and legal, accusing the Indians of piracy. By the end of 2001, however, all the bad publicity and angry people in the streets shamed Big Pharma into allowing the manufacture of generics in Africa and selling their products at reduced prices. Activists insist that the drugs remain far too pricey for most people with AIDS in poor countries, and that more assistance is required.

But let's go back to the patent—and hanging on to it at all costs. If all the legal and semilegal stalling doesn't work, makers unveil an ostensibly improved version of the old drug. Claritin is trumped by Clarinex. Prilosec, the original purple pill, gives way to today's purple pill, Nexium. The other way to hang on to your patent is to find a new use for the old drug. Lilly tried to stave off the horrors of patent expiration by rebranding its greatest hit, Prozac, as Sarafem, a cure for premenstrual dysmorphic disorder. PMDD is basically PMS Turbo. PMS has always mystified me, not because it doesn't exist, but because it does, and almost every woman I have met in my life has some twinge or symptom of it. And the stats back up my anecdotal tales of gal pals having backaches or bursting into tears; about two-thirds of women are affected. This makes me wonder how anything that afflicts that much of a given population can possibly be considered a disease. Aren't the minority of the sisterhood who flounce through the month unhindered the anomalous ones? If almost everybody feels something to the point where it is the stuff of coffee-mug and T-shirt slogans, then surely it is not a disorder, but normal—a thing simply to be endured, and tamed with the usual low-grade anodynes.

Lilly insisted that PMDD, Xtreme PMS, was downright debilitating, and sold Sarafem with the classic pitch-to-the-ladies, the empowerment message, encouraging women to liberate themselves from the tyranny of bloat and moods. The ads for the little lavender and pink pills encourage gals to "be more like the woman you are." Lilly got its knuckles rapped by the FDA for one ad in particular. It showed a young woman struggling unsuccessfully, and with increasing hysteria, with a fiendishly uncooperative grocery cart. The FDA argued that the ad trivialized the disorder, which strikes me as pretty funny, considering that the whole point of Lilly's campaign was to give PMDD the gravitas of a disease so that they could supply the cure.

Paxil, never far behind Prozac, took a similar tack with a campaign about social anxiety disorder, and then generalized anxiety disorder, providing shiny new diseases for a drug known primarily as an antidepressant. In case you aren't up on your disorders, those are Turbo Shyness and Xtreme Jitters, respectively. Many pharmaceutical marketing campaigns don't sell the cure. They sell the disease, identifying a cluster of symptoms and giving them a name. And once a company finds a best-selling malaise, they start marketing all the adjacent feelings. Depression begets a host of anxiety and panic disorders. Viagra and Cialis prove an astounding success, and so we are treated, or soon will be, to campaigns about the scourge that is female sexual dysfunction.

This is not to discount the genuine therapeutic benefits of prescription drugs, which have helped people recover from debilitating conditions. Depression is bloody awful, and if Prozac can shake you out of it, more power to you and Lilly and your caring clinicians. But it's not as easy to diagnose a depression as it is to spot a tumor or a blood pressure problem. There's no way to really test people for many of the disorders for which antidepressants are prescribed, other than some shrinky-dinky quizzes, which seem to get more and more general with each passing drug. CNN recently did a spot on a new drug for attention deficit disorder called Strattera. The anchors joked about the website's diagnostic questions: Do you feel unfocused, disorganized, or restless? Yes! Are you unable to concentrate on any one thing for any length of time? So true! Meanwhile, the crawl beneath the picture carried the latest blips about Bush and Laci Peterson, while the current temperatures and sports scores flashed in another corner and, in the background, more monitors blinked. Who could focus on anything for any length of time? The Lilly website even compares the condition to a "channel [that] keeps changing in your mind and you don't have control of the remote."

The snappier turnaround times demanded by an overburdened health care system mean that way too many doctor appointments are little more than ill-defined complaints and pitches for a quick fix. You tell 'em you feel like six pounds of shit in a five-pound bag and that you've heard of this new miracle cure, and then they hand you a couple of sample packs, a pamphlet, and a scrip. The laundry list of disorders for which antidepressants are prescribed has increased and now includes everything from body dysmorphic disorder to posttraumatic stress disorder to gambling, shopping, and sex addictions. And every one of these relatively new disorders has enjoyed at least fifteen minutes of fame, often in the form of designated celebrity sufferers, magazine spreads, or a very special day on *The Oprah Winfrey Show* or *Dr. Phil.*

Feeling like six pounds of shit in a five-pound bag is nothing new. There have been melancholias and manias on the medical books since the Ancient Greeks. In a more churchy time, these symptoms might have been interpreted as demonic possession and treated with exorcism, or maybe a trepanning, or perhaps a good bleeding to get your humors back in working order. In the early days of psychoanalysis, the same symptoms might have been evidence of a neurosis or a block, and the patient would have had to talk his or her way through it, in search of primordial trauma, perhaps under the influence of hypnosis or cocaine. Over the course of the last century, doctors developed brutal surgical interventions like lobotomies to try to tame mental illness, but pharmaceuticals have been the preferred form of treatment since the seventies.

The first few classes of antidepressants, the tricyclics and the MAOIs, had rotten side effects like dry mouth, blurry vision, sweating, and severe, sometimes fatal, allergic reactions that discouraged their widespread use.

It was not until the early nineties that things began to change. In the post-Prozac world, a World Health Organization study on depression estimated that 121 million people suffered from the disorder, and that only a quarter of them had access to treatment. Now I hate to make chicken and egg arguments, but which came first, the miracle cures or the global depression epidemic? My money's on the cures. Since the new, ostensibly side-effect-free SSRIs became available, the number of people who seek treatment for depression has tripled, and the use of antidepressants has more than doubled. Hell, I've taken one, too. Paxil was another one of those drugs that I did briefly, and didn't much care to continue doing. I took it for a couple of months, until I wasn't freaking out anymore, and then stopped because it made me feel fizzy, numb, and wired. I know plenty of people, more cranky than crazy, who have also given one of the SSRIs a whirl, and I suspect you know a few, too.

According to a report by the American Medical Association, part of the reason for this is the increased public profile of such drugs, as well as the general destigmatization of mental illness. Once upon a time you might have kept your mad relatives in the attic, away from prying eyes; now we blab in locker rooms and chat rooms about our meds. The shift was suspiciously sudden. Granted, the freedom to discuss our own bouts of insanity seems an improvement over locking ourselves or our loved ones up, but it also testifies to the awesome power of marketing.

Are millions of us really that fucked-up? And if, indeed, the fucked-up are legion, then shouldn't we be sniffing around for the reasons behind the depression epidemic? Either way you look at it, it's pretty depressing. Millions of people may well be taking drugs they don't need to clear up a medical condition that is nothing more than a glorified bad mood. On the other hand, millions of men, women, and children might be seriously ill for reasons we don't understand, and might find themselves dependent on drugs, with all the side effects, long-term effects, and costs that situation implies. Take your pick: a massive snake-oil swindle or a ginormous public health crisis.

SSRIs clearly have their uses. For those afflicted with severe depression, the four food groups and a daily stroll will not suffice. However, I suspect that too many people label themselves depressed and turn to pills too quickly, since they provide the promise of a much easier fix than the kind of lifestyle changes that actually lead to better physical and mental health. If your day consists of sitting in a car snorting fumes, sitting in front of a computer screen, sitting in a car again, and then sitting in front of a television screen while grazing on all manner of toxins and worrying intermittently about your debts, your job, and your relationships, then it is little wonder you do not feel very good. You should not feel good. That pain is your body saying quit it with the shitty life. Doing the good-health thing requires rearranging your schedule, which you might not have the leeway and resources to do, and waiting a while for the effects to kick in. With a pill, you just buy it and swallow it. We're good at buying and swallowing.

If you look at the top killers in the U.S.—heart disease, stroke, cancer, chronic lower respiratory disease, pneumonia/influenza, liver disease—you will see that there is not one blockbuster pill that cures any of them. There are some peripherals, sure, to keep your cholesterol down and maybe help with the heart. But most of these diseases spring from a lifetime of bad habits. These are the diseases of a stressed-out people who do not get enough exercise, eat too much lousy food, and marinate in a soup of chemicals. So when the works inevitably begin to rot, why not throw more chemicals into the mix? Fire with fire, baby. Here's another list: the top ten global pharmaceuticals in 2003 were Lipitor, Zocor, Zyprexa, Norvasc, Procrit, Prevacid, Nexium, Plavix, Advair, and Zoloft, for cholesterol, cholesterol, depression, hypertension, anemia, heartburn, heartburn, blood clots, asthma, and depression, respectively. The list of mortality leaders and wonder drugs doesn't match up as nicely as one might hope it would. Throw in estrogen therapy, antibiotics, painkillers, Accutane, and Viagra, and that about sums it up for the fifty best-selling drugs, which account for half of all drug sales.

We take pills to chase away the erosions and abrasions of our bad habits, not to cure any of the illnesses that actually dispatch us to the worm farm. It's like Chris Rock said: "There ain't no money in the cure." All drug dealers, from the CEOs of Big Pharma to the kingpins of the illegal trade, are looking not for the cure, but for the chronic, the product the junkie needs a little bit of every day for the rest of his or her life. There's a pill for every age of man, and every complaint that accompanies that age. The fidgeting and flightiness of youth can be curbed with Ritalin, or Strattera, or some other copycat version of speed for kids. The miseries and confusion of adolescence and early adulthood can be managed with one of the SSRIs. If the spuds are looking runty, you can start them on a course of Humatrope, the growth hormone, so they can get in on the benefits of a few extra inches. The wear and tear of middle age can be assuaged with your Celebrexes, your Prilosecs and your Nexiums. And your golden years will involve, more likely than not, handfuls of pills, so many pills that some of them will be pills you take simply to counteract your other pills.

We may be caught up in healthism, but we are far from healthy. Half of us North Americans are obese. Even as the prescriptions and the AbTronics and ginkgo biloba fairly walk off the shelves, our obesity rates continue to rise, and obesity is right up there with smoking as a grievous mortality factor and preventable cause of disease.

A pill doesn't change your habits. It's just another habit, another product to add to your daily regime of consumption, another chemical introduced into the mix of chemicals. People used to take pills either as a matter of the utmost medical exigency, or to liven up a night on the dance floor. Now people take pills simply to be themselves. Paxil encourages you to see someone you haven't seen in a while—namely, you. It's natural to be chemical. And, as anyone who has done drugs knows, doing drugs is the leading cause of doing more drugs. You either develop a dependency and need more of the same old shit to feel it, or the first drug leads you to other drugs. Conservatives love to talk about the gateway effect when it comes to illegal drugs. Smoke a joint, and you're on the road to junkiedom. But nobody breathes a word about the gateway effect of prescription drugs. I can't help but wonder how many of those eager Prilosec consumers are taking it to soothe their burnt-out Prozac guts.

CHAPTER SEVEN

THE BEST POLICY

In Which Your Humble Correspondent Confesses to Being Totally Baffled by the Entire Insurance Industry

Insurance: n. *An ingenious modern game of chance in which the player is permitted to enjoy the comfortable conviction that he is beating the man who keeps the table.*

—AMBROSE BIERCE

In January of 2005, Marsh & McLennan, one of the biggest insurance brokers in the United States, agreed to pay $850 million to settle charges that they had engaged in bid-rigging and taken kickbacks. Marsh was supposed to find insurance plans for companies, but they faked wildly inflated bids to sell mildly inflated bids, and then got commissions from the insurers, who benefited from the cunning little scheme. They would neither confirm nor deny these allegations, of course, but they agreed to pay, apologize, and mend their wicked ways. New York State Attorney General Eliot Spitzer, who led the Marsh probe, has been handing out sheaves of subpoenas to insurers, alleging widespread corruption throughout the industry. Nobody bid-rigs alone, and bid-rigging is but one of the infractions investigators are considering. Aon, ACE, AIG, Aetna, Cigna, Hartford, and MetLife are some of the giant

American insurers who are the objects of Spitzer's latest blitz. Though his detractors claim that this is another well-publicized crusade en route to his impending campaign for governor, attorneys general in other states, like California and Connecticut, are following Spitzer's lead, and have also started issuing subpoenas to insurance companies.

I don't think Spitzer's insurance probe is a Machiavellian ploy, but if it is, it is a damn good one. I think a lot of people are wondering where, exactly, their premiums go, particularly when those premiums are rising precipitously. The most hotly contested issue in recent elections in my neighborhood, specifically Nova Scotia and New Brunswick, was car insurance. People were pissed about double-digit premium increases, and they demanded that all the candidates speak to this issue. Some demanded that the candidates commit to the establishment of public auto insurance, as they have in Saskatchewan and Manitoba. Others demanded that the candidates pass legislation curbing the outrageous rate hikes. The Nova Scotia government ended up negotiating a soft-tissue injury claim cap in exchange for lesser increases, a decidedly industry-friendly solution. In February of 2005, when the Canadian insurance industry reported making a record-breaking $4 billion in profit in 2004, the headlines, even in staid papers, used words like *obscene* and *outrage*.

This insurance ire is one example of the resentment that smolders in the hearts of policyholders across this great landmass. The insurance industry may not be as obviously synonymous with bullshit as advertising or politics, but people are becoming more and more frustrated with its escalating costs and baffling verbiage, given that they have to have insurance if they want a house or a car or, in the United States, to not die. Lawyers have been milking insurance rage for a long time. Insurers are being sued in scores of suits, class action and individual, meritorious and spurious. The Web fairly teems with sad stories by the screwed. Folks stuck at home, sick and waiting for a settlement, have all the time in the world to put up Web sites detailing wildly ungrammatical tales of their insurers' hardheartedness, ranging from failure to pay for repairs and medical care to denying or delaying benefits and stalking of policyholders who have submitted claims. The industry, for its part, claims that premium increases have everything to do with the dot-com market bust, costs associated with September 11, ridiculously generous jury awards, and fraud on the part of malingerers. They have nothing to do with their billion-dollar profit margins.

The rage may be relatively new, but insurance is hardly a new kid on the bullshit block. It's almost as old as misfortune itself. Maritime cultures going back to the Babylonians had some form of risk pool to cover expenses stemming from the hazards of trading missions. If the boats sailed off the edge of the world into the gullet of a sea serpent, someone had to cover the loss of cargo, craft, and crew. Lloyd's of London, the most venerable of the world's insurers, set up shop in a coffee-house in London in the late 1600s to do just this. Wealthy patrons signed their names at the end of a contract outlining how much risk they were willing to undertake. This is where we get the term *underwriter,* one of the many archaisms preserved in the wordy world of insurance. Insurance set up shop in the colonies early. Benjamin Franklin was one of the founding fathers of the Philadelphia Contributorship for the Insurance of Houses from Loss by Fire, one of America's first insurance companies, chartered in 1752. The actuarial set have had a long time to refine their arts and have cooked up a field of endeavor that, when practiced irresponsibly, is the el nacho grande king hell scam of all scams. Because you, dear policyholder, don't have to understand the arcane lexicon of insurance or even read your interminable and inscrutable policy; no, you just have to buy it.

Don't get me wrong. I have no quibble with the notion of a risk pool, or with people investing the interest from the funds in that risk pool. Like the corporation, insurance is a good way to accumulate capital for risky ventures. We need insurance to keep jets in the air, boats on the water, and companies in business. Most of the remaining public-spirited government programs are effectively insurance programs, safety nets that kick in when misfortune befalls you. This is how commercial insurance markets itself, but do not mistake insurers for public trusts, even though the product the insurer is selling to the public, is, for all intents and purposes, trust. Insurance isn't a product like a frosty Coke, or a service like getting your hair done. Instead, you pay the insurer for the promise of a service or a settlement, in the event that you require it. It's a gamble.

Most people buy insurance hoping they will never need it, fearing that they might. Almost every soft, squishy, vulnerable being with a few affectionate ties and a reasonable accumulation of possessions has a reptilian spot in their brain that houses panic, the fear that they will lose it all. Sure, you can whistle while you work, and saunter down the sunny side of the street, but even optimists know full well that you could roll your leased SUV on a cruddy stretch of highway and be a vegetable for the rest of your days. What would the spouse and kids do then, hmmm? How about a house fire? Care for a cancer?

All this scary shit is the sweet spot for insurers, the little nub of fear the industry massages with its actuarial fingers until the money flows. "Buy a policy," says the soothing voice of insurance, "and we'll take care of everything." Besides, if the fear don't move you to buy insurance, the bankers and the law will. You have to have insurance to have the big-ticket things. Your bank will demand insurance as a condition of the mortgage, since it's their house, in effect. Auto insurance enjoys the distinction of being something people must purchase by law. Even if you don't have a house or a car, and don't own much of anything, you're still dragging around that perishable carcass of yours. And when unfortunate Americans need appendectomies, or are midway through massive coronaries, it can't help to have to wonder how much the fucker is going to cost.

Insurers do not wish any ill upon their customers. Au contraire: they are your friend, your neighbor, your little piece of the rock, the good-hands people, the ones who'll be there, check in hand, after your house vanishes up a funnel. They want to see you hale and hearty and frolicking in a meadow of wildflowers with your loved ones. If insurance companies had their druthers, all their cherished policyholders would be fire-retardant, impeccable motorists, immune to everything, and immortal, but unaware of their superpowers. Insurance companies shake the money out of your pockets by promising to take care of you, but they only get to keep that money if you don't require any care. Let me run that by you one more time, since it blows my tiny mind: Their profits depend on policyholders not demanding the money formerly known as theirs.

An insurance policy is a wager, and the insurance industry is a Las Vegas of morbidity and misery. Insurers look at risk factors (your health, age, lineage, and demographic wedge) the same way a poker champion eyeballs your body language and all the cards he can see, calculating odds based on available information. If you're holding a crappy hand—family history of cancer, a string of drunk-driving convictions, a two-pack-a-day habit—insurers charge you higher premiums. Of course, once you are insured, the quickest way to make it clear that you present an undesirable level of risk is to actually file a claim. If you have the temerity to require the care you've been paying premiums for, you can expect those premiums to shoot up. After all, nothing shows an unseemly taste for an extravagance like medical care quite like actually needing medical care. This is what makes insurance a totally perverse commodity. Deductibles and premium increases after claims filings mean that it is often cheaper to pay for the garage or the stitches yourself. That is certainly way cheaper for the insurance company, too. They call it "customers assuming responsibility for their own risk management."

In the States, the insurance industry has two underwriting branches, property-casualty and life-health. P&C covers car crashes, house fires, and hurricanes; L&H handles your checkups, your cancer, and your coffin. In the Great White North, as you well know, basic health is covered by taxes, not premiums, but we still have private prescription, dental, life, and P&C. In the U.S., the P&C sector is not regulated by federal law. Insurance companies are regulated by an uneven patchwork of state laws, and they've lobbied since the forties to keep it that way. Through the nineties, property and casualty was the less lucrative of the two sectors, thanks to more sales and higher prices for life and health insurance. Annuities—life insurance policies that involve an investment component—were the fastest-growing insurance product, reflecting the stock-mad sensibility of the times and the anxieties of an aging population. Over the decade, annuities sold so well that they caught up with, and then sped past, total premiums for auto insurance. Annuities are also pricier than the product they tended to replace, term life, and the switchover was a boon for the industry. Health insurance prices have been increasing steadily since 1989. Premiums have gone up by at least 10 percent a year every year since 2001.

At the same time, in the P&C sector, too many companies were selling insurance for any one company to make a truly sweet profit. This is, by the way, one of the many reasons why your premiums will be going nowhere but up, up, up for the next couple of years. Welcome to the underwriting cycle, where prices tend to fluctuate every three to five years. When there was a highly competitive market during the nineties investment boom, underwriters sold P&C policies at slashed premium rates to get as many customers signed up as possible, effectively saturating the market with inexpensive policies. Hey, you can always jack those premiums up once people have signed on the dotted line—which is precisely what they'll be doing for the next few years, since the property and casualty business claims that it has just had a few shitty years.

The year 2004 was awful, thanks to a succession of hurricanes, resulting in over $20 billion in claims. Thanks to September 11, 2001 was bad too, the most expensive single disaster the insurance industry has ever had to cope with. The attack affected many sectors of the insurance industry, from life to property to aviation liability. The industry's latest estimates show that insurers are on the hook for about $40 billion in claims. This is more than double the most expensive natural disaster, Hurricane Andrew, which cost them about $15 billion. Insurers briefly entertained invoking the act of war clause to dodge the costs, since the president was referring to terrorism as war, but they soon realized that this probably wouldn't survive a court challenge, or the court of public opinion. Fortunately, over a hundred companies carried a portion of the costs, so only a couple went down in flames, primarily aviation underwriters. Reinsurance, or insurers insuring insurers, has played a crucial role in spreading the costs of September 11, as reinsurers are in for over half of the projected costs.

Insurers successfully lobbied the government for "back-stop" funds to help meet their financial obligations without imperiling their liquidity or reserves, and they also pushed for a terrorism exemption. Though the act of war exemption, an industry standard since the nineteenth century, was verbally loose enough to fit September 11 because it includes acts of undeclared war, the industry pushed for a clause specifically excluding terrorism. Both demands became law in 2002, in the form of the Terrorism Risk Insurance Act. This means that taxpayers, rather than insurers, will bear the majority of the cost of future terrorism. Policy renewals no longer cover acts of terror, or specifically exclude chemical, biological, and nuclear acts of terror. The exclusion was important to the industry not just to decrease their risk exposure, but to secure the silver lining of all of these terrorism costs—a burgeoning market in expensive terrorism coverage packages. It's the genius of capitalism!

Free-marketeers love to make the choice argument, and extol our absolute freedom to buy. The choice argument kind of hits the fan with a bizarro product like insurance. Do people really choose to get insurance? Um, no. When people go for retail therapy, they buy shoes, video games, and ice cream, not term life. While you are free to choose your insurer, you only get insurance if they choose you. Once you have insurance, what are your choices, should they refuse your claim? Well, you can choose to pursue an internal appeal, or sue, at which point they will probably choose to drag out the jeezly claim for as long as is bureaucratically possible. Yes sir, a whole lot of choice going on there.

Insurance, be it property and casualty, or life and health, is a textbook example of an inefficient market, where there is little incentive for any provider in the system to offer lower prices or better service. The market share is pretty much captive. It's difficult for buyers to do any comparison shopping when selecting a policy, as their selections may be limited by their employer or by the bank that holds their mortgage. Once they sign up, people tend not to switch policies because they do not want to be underwritten again. Besides, people only find out that their insurer's services are bad the hard way: by paying their premiums for years, and then being denied service or dropped unceremoniously or gouged relentlessly when shit comes to shovel.

Prose-wise, both types of insurance policies hail from Boredom Square, in the heart of downtown Dullsville. Any bureaucracy's first line of defense is verbiage that fairly repels its readers, a blend of bafflegab, boilerplate, loopholes, and jargon. The industry blames the fine print and legalese on lawyers, their natural enemies and favorite scapegoats. Outrageous jury awards, most of which march into the coffers of the aforementioned lawyers, are often cited as a reason for escalating premium costs, and the insurance industry is an ardent supporter of tort reform. The pas de deux between the standing armies of U.S. lawyers and insurers is fascinating: two behemoths locked in pitched battle for the pockets of the people, churning up an unholy cloud of obfuscating bafflegab, both claiming that they toil in Joe Policyholder's best interest. The insurance companies' necessarily deep capital reserves are an irresistible lure for any lawyer. It's not just the personal injury lawyers with 1–800 numbers for whiplash victims that hound the industry. Insurance companies make great targets for class action suits, too, and lawyers love the millions that can be made from these suits. But it was the insurance industry that helped make the legal monster. It's pretty disingenuous to sign contracts with millions of Americans, honor said contracts with varying forthrightness and zeal, and then wonder why everyone's gotten so bloody litigious. Still, the insurance lobby speaks as though every suit were yet another fraudulent raid on its vaults, led by self-interested ambulance chasers who pocket most of the obscene settlements themselves.

There's no love lost on the legal side: most of the anti-insurance sites on the Web are about individual or class action suits against insurers. Insurance companies bought some of these domain names themselves, like "state-farm-sucks.com," in a bold preemptive strike against bad word-of-Web, but there are still scads of complaint sites with stories of ongoing or impending litigation. Some suits claim that insurers act in bad faith by using stall tactics to delay payments and deny claims, or have focused on other breach of contract issues, like premium rates that double and triple within a year of purchasing a supposedly low-cost policy. This is a bait-and-switch; they sell you a plan that seems comprehensive and affordable, but then the insurer raises the rates, or reduces the coverage, once you have committed to the plan. And it's not just policy-holders who are suing insurance providers, either. Doctors have filed suit against health care giants like Cigna and Aetna, claiming the health care providers are engaged in corrupt practices like "bundling" and "downcoding." Bundling is lumping several services together, a strategy to pay doctors less in fees; downcoding is paying for cheaper procedures than the ones the doctors actually performed.

We'll come back to those lawsuits—there are plenty to choose from—but first let's look at how private health insurance actually works. The health and life business is an even more arcane, complex, bureaucratic behemoth than property and casualty. It is also a business that has changed completely over the past twenty years. Most health insurance plans used to work according to a system called fee-for-service, which is how the public insurance system in Canada still works. Your doctor would recommend treatments, and your insurer would pick up the bill. Over the past two decades, U.S. insurers have switched to two different types of managed care insurance plans, the health maintenance organization (HMO) and the preferred provider organization (PPO). HMO plans require that you see only approved practitioners, and may refuse to pay for treatments performed by someone else. PPOs, the more costly option, allow you greater freedom of choice when choosing practitioners. Both HMOs and PPOs do more than provide insurance; HMOs and PPOs often include hospitals, doctors, other health care providers, and several tiers of administrative middlemen, all rolled into one big megacorp.

In both HMOs and PPOs, the doctors receive a flat fee for each patient. This is called capitation, and if it seems benign, bear in mind that what it means is that a capitated doctor makes less money every time he recommends an expensive treatment. The kid with the sniffles is pure profit; the triple-bypass patient gnaws away at the bottom line. And even if you happen to be Mr. or Ms. Hero Doctor, who still holds the Hippocratic Oath in higher esteem than the bottom line, you are but a gatekeeper in the managed care process. You can refer patients to specialists, and you can suggest radical treatment options, but in the end the decision will not be made by you or, for that matter, by your patient. Such decisions rest in the capable hands of a middleman.

Most Americans rely on their employers for health care coverage. Employers pick up the health insurance tab for 60 percent of the Americans who have coverage, and they have been trying, desperately, to reduce their swelling insurance costs. Employers are making employees responsible for larger portions of their health care costs through higher co-pays and deductibles. Those without an employer-provided health plan can buy private plans, but they are more costly than plans negotiated at a group rate. The government, through the auspices of Medicaid and Medicare, provides some care for the approximately 40 million people covered by each program. These funds are primarily for the old, children, and the very poor. Medicaid and Medicare have also been trying to reduce their costs and improve their services by enrolling people in managed care, but the program hasn't been as successful as the feds hoped it might be; enrolees have had rising out-of-pocket costs, and HMOs have been dropping out of the program in droves. The government just doesn't pay 'em enough.

More than 45 million Americans, many of them full-time workers, have no health insurance coverage whatsoever. The uninsured tend not to do things like go to doctors, or seek preventative care, but they can visit hospital emergency rooms. Hospitals risk fines for "dumping" if they turn away patients in severe distress who fail the wallet biopsy, but emergency care hardly serves as a substitute for actual health coverage. Patients are still billed, and face much higher costs, even for routine procedures, than they would if they were visiting regular clinicians. Whether you are covered or have no coverage at all, ill health is the leading cause of financial ruin, accounting for half of U.S. bankruptcies.

The U.S. is the globe's undisputed leader in health care costs. It has the most expensive health care system in the world. Yet, in terms of access to care, the U.S. lags well behind other nations. The 2000 World Health Report, issued by the World Health

Organization, focused on the issue of health delivery systems, and compared their costs and benefits. The U.S. placed twenty-fourth in overall health system attainment, nestled between Israel and Cyprus. In terms of fairness of financial contribution to the health system, the U.S. drops further still, to 54—just ahead of Fiji and prewar Iraq. The U.S. health care system is expensive in part because of advances in technology and increased usage of prescription drugs, the better stuff and the shinier things. But health care is also wildly expensive because it is a poorly organized market, full of high-paid middlemen.

It's one thing to make a loopy, litigious system like insurance into a surtax on niceties like owning a house or a car. Oh, sure, it keeps the working poor from movin' on up to the middle class, but you can rent and take the bus until you have enough money for insurance and a house or a car. It might be inconvenient, but you won't die. But it's quite another thing to marry and mate the colossus of insurance with the business of saving lives. People do die, sometimes needlessly and awfully. I'm one of those loons who think health care should be available to everyone and paid for by taxes, like it is in Canada and most other Western nations. There should be no co-pay, no deductible, no bureaucracies devoted to the bean-counting of care. It's not just that it would be more ethical; it would probably be cheaper, too. Seriously. It's no wonder that the American health care system is the priciest, what with lawyers and bureaucrats doing nothing but regulating access to care. Not providing care, not curing jack, just filing forms and more forms, haggling about who gets what when—and clogging up the legal system to boot. At least under so-called socialized medicine, there's just one horde of civil-service bureaucrats squabbling among themselves, and fewer lawsuits. Under privatized medicine with some state care, there are actually three nonmedical groups at work: the

insurers, the lawyers, and all the civil servants you still end up
hiring. One study, published in *The New England Journal of
Medicine* in 2003, showed that public health systems actually
had much lower administrative costs than private ones. The
United States spends three times as much money per capita on
health care administration than Canadians do under a public,
single-payer system. Administrative costs eat up almost a third
of U.S. health spending. Canada's administrative costs are half
that, at 16 percent of health spending.

Remember those public auto insurance systems in Saskatchewan and Manitoba I mentioned way back when? It
turns out that the Canadian provinces with public insurance
have far more stable premium rates than the ones with private
systems. There have been some increases, most notably in
Quebec, but these increases have been modest compared to
the skyrocketing rates in provinces with private systems. In
Manitoba, premium increases for 2002 were 1.8 percent, well
below the 26 percent increase in neighboring Alberta, or the
over 30 percent increases in the Maritime Provinces. Manitoba
Public Insurance is the cheapest in the nation, and it also de-
votes a greater percentage of premium income to paying out
claims—90 percent, as opposed to the industry rate of 73 percent. MPI is also financially solvent and self-sufficient, lest you
envision a taxpayer-funded boondoggle.

Of course, public auto insurance isn't on the table in the
U.S., nor is any form of public health insurance. Call me a
commie, or hopelessly Canadian, but you can't tell me it isn't
feasible for the state to provide some basic health care for
everyone. It's the least they can do for your tax dollar, and it's
the sort of thing that states do better than corporations. The
classic lefty argument is that the health of the nation should
not rest in the hands of people who make decisions based on

the short-term exigencies of the profit motive. But you can also make this argument in market-friendly terms: health care costs are an onerous burden free enterprise should not have to bear. *The Economist* has been singing Canada's praises lately, rating it the best country in the world in which to do business, and Canada's public infrastructure is part of the reason this is so. There are plenty of American companies up here, happy not to pay health premiums.

Of course, this is all wildly utopian. I might as well propose a public program providing free pie on Fridays as argue that health care needs be public. I can reel off stats and studies and sad stories, but the grim fact remains: There are plenty of lobbies devoted to keeping medical care a strictly private and profitable matter. No self-respecting multibillion-dollar industry is going to say, "Take our billions and fire us en masse! We will beat our clipboards into plowshares and till the earth—please spend the billions on the cancer patients and the house fire victims and the sufferers of vehicular malaise!" This is not how industries become and remain multibillion-dollar industries. Private health care is a fucked-up fact of American life, and the profiteers are creeping into Canada, too. Why, even Hillary's doomed, supposedly socialist, health care plan only suggested that the government act as a sort of health care broker, negotiating with a consortium of existing health care providers to obtain care. That modest proposal was received like so much commie talk. I admit that it is an odd proposition, the whole state-trusting thing. But, sadly, the only thing that strikes me as even crazier is to leave it in the hands of a ginormous corporation. Capitated as a covered life by my gatekeeper? Thanks, but no thanks.

Terms like *capitation* and *gatekeeper* are but a smidge of the heady lingua franca that is all insurance's own. Do you know what a "death spiral" is? It's what starts to happen once a policy pool is closed and its members start to age. Premiums go up, and healthy members of the pool opt out and head for cheaper coverage, driving premiums up. Even at higher premiums, the pool is less profitable, because it has selected out all the healthy pure-profit types who offset the cost of the invalids. And because rising premium costs do not keep pace with the pool's needs, the pool has to reduce its expenditures. Ergo, people pay more, and get less care, at a point in their lives when they need care most. The death spiral is actuarial entropy, and the only way to avoid it is to not sign up too many sickies in the first place. Insurers try not to get locked in a death spiral with preventative measures like cherry-picking, also known as "creaming," which means insuring only those people who don't have much need for insurance, and letting the risky folks trickle down into state-funded programs like Medicare. You may recognize this strategy from successful industries such as banking and energy, which rack up record-breaking profits even as they leave record-breaking messes behind for taxpayer-funded agencies to clean up. Only this time, the mess is people. Sick people.

Managed care organizations have also been accused of shorting doctors to cut costs. Doctors have had some success pursuing HMOs for racketeering. Richard Scruggs, the lawyer largely responsible for Big Tobacco class action suits, got the ball rolling in Miami in 1999. Since then, a few major HMO class action suits have been winding their way through the courts. In one class action, *Shane et al vs. Humana*, Aetna agreed to a $120 million settlement in October 2004 to prevent a suit alleging they used automatic payment systems, among other forms of chicanery, to underpay doctors. Cigna, another big health insurer named in the suit, agreed to a settlement of $85 million. Another class action suit alleging similar violations, *United Health Group vs. Klay,* was approved by the Supreme Court in January 2005. The Supremes rejected the insurer's pleas that the class of thousands of health care professionals from several states was too loose to sue. However, the class shouldn't stock up on champagne just yet. Right after that, the Bush admin achieved one of its tort-reforming goals: class action suits now proceed to federal courts, rather than state courts, as state courts have been more lavish with punitive damages, and they tend to be more sympathetic than federal courts have been to those screwed by insurance.

Some states have lobbied for a patient's right to sue. Texas, for example, has a law that permits patients to sue their insurers. This right to sue became law in 1997, back when Dubya was governor, before he converted to the gospel of tort reform. A 2004 Supreme Court decision, in the case of *Aetna vs. Davila,* decreed that the Texas state law was overruled by a federal law called the Employee Retirement Income Security Act (ERISA), passed in 1974. ERISA was intended to regulate the managers of funds, and to protect the assets of the employees contributing to pension or health insurance funds. But ERISA was written before HMOs became so prevalent, and the act preempts employee rights to sue their health care provider for denial of necessary care. *Aetna vs. Davila* is just the latest in a series of attempts by lawyers to prove that care managers have run afoul of ERISA by denying medical benefits to policyholders. In the *Davila* decision, the Supremes mentioned the precedent set by a 2000 case called *Pegram vs. Herdrich.* A patient named Cynthia Herdrich sued her doctor and her HMO for making her wait for care for a stomach pain that turned into a ruptured appendix. Herdrich argued that this denial of care was a breach of fiduciary duty under ERISA. The Supreme Court ultimately ruled that the cost-containment measures used by

HMOs did not constitute a breach of ERISA statutes, and that, furthermore, to rule that they did would pretty much put HMOs out of business, since they all use the same cost-containment measures.

The managed care battle isn't taking place just in the courts. Patients' rights legislation has also been on the federal agenda since Clinton. In August of 2001, after many adjustments and a muchness of negotiation, the Senate and House finally passed patients' rights legislation, amending ERISA to respond to issues specific to HMOs. The sticking point amid all the bipartisan compromising was the right to sue, and how much people could sue for. The Democrats, who do very well by trial lawyers donation-wise, were generous in that regard. The Republicans, who receive more from insurance companies and the financial services lobby, took the line that the right to sue would drive up premium costs. The bill allows patients a limited right to sue, but not until all other avenues are exhausted. The lawsuit must be approved by an outside adjudicator, so as to discourage flights of legal frivolity. The law also caps punitive damages at $1.5 million. Bush wanted to limit that to $500,000, but had to concede to the higher cap to keep rogue Republicans on side. Needless to say, the industry claimed the new law would only serve to increase premiums and the number of uninsured, which just goes to show what you get when you let the dead hand of regulation tickle the market.

Patients' rights legislation may well be a bee in the industry's bonnet, but I think that there is another piece of legislation out there that is having a far more profound effect on the industry. In 1999, the Gramm-Leach-Bliley Financial Services Modernization Act repealed barriers that had held bankers, securities dealers, and insurance companies at arm's length from one another since the Glass-Steagall Act of 1933. I'm going to refer to the GLB act, aka the FMA, as the Glob, since it essentially gathers all forms of financial services, including insurance, together into one great blobby Glob. Part of the impetus for the Glob was the Federal Reserve's decision the year before to approve a merger between Citibank and Travelers insurance. The merger, which produced behemoth Citigroup, has been touted as the future of financial services, a sort of supermarket where you can shop for your stocks, checks, and insurance policies. Of course, there were good reasons why, in 1933, people reckoned that particular convenience wasn't worth the risk, but sixty-odd years later, all that total economic collapse jive was so much ancient history. It was time for the legislation to catch up with the industry, and the industry doesn't seem to mind federal regulation when it favors them, or when it frees them from the burden of state laws. The Glob preempts state laws about banks merging with insurers, or cross-selling insurance; states have the option of enforcing stricter laws, but at the implicit cost of insurers hightailing it to slacker states.

Cross-selling is big business, and another side effect of the legislation is a glorious information-sharing. Insurers are starting to use credit checks as part and parcel of the underwriting process, and privacy advocates are howling about how the consolidation of the financial services industry makes this much easier for insurers. The Glob also ferries your premium dollar ever further into the casino economy of speculation. The kind of convergence that the Glob encourages has been creeping up on us for a while. In 1991, one of California's largest insurance companies, Executive Life, was sold to a front company for a group of French investors that included bank Credit Lyonnais. The sale violated state law, as it was illegal for a bank, particularly a foreign bank, to buy a California insurer.

The French investors' group had no interest in running an insurance company, but they had to take the company to get their hands on its bond portfolio. They paid only $3.5 billion for the insurance operation and its bond portfolio, even though the bonds alone were ostensibly worth about $6 billion. The California attorney general estimates that 300,000 policyholders lost $4 billion in coverage after the sale and subsequent collapse of Executive Life.

You may not recognize the name of the man who helped broker the sale for the illegal investors. His name is Leon Black, and he still runs an investment company called the Apollo Group, which participated in the Executive Life deal and helped channel the bonds into a bunch of French fronts that also began with the letter A, like Altus and Artemis. You may not know Black, but you are probably familiar with his former co-worker and crony at Drexel Burnham Lambert: Mike Milken. Milken called the sale of Executive Life "the investment opportunity of the decade" in a 1992 jailhouse interview with *Forbes* magazine. The junk bond crash, fueled in part by Milken's indictment and the Drexel investigation, meant that Executive Life was sitting on a lot of cheap assets. Black and the French investors made a killing on the bonds once the junk scare subsided. In 1999, after complaints from angry policyholders, the attorney general and the insurance commissioner filed suit against those involved in the Executive Life deal. In 2002, Black and his associates agreed to testify against the French in exchange for immunity. In 2005, after beaucoup de international legal wrangling, the French investors involved in the suit paid over $600 million to settle the case.

What I find sadly funny about this sordid tale is that the insurance industry won't sell somebody a measly policy because they've got diabetes or a DUI, but somehow, someone with a great weeping ethical sore like "Mike Milken's Right-Hand Man" on his CV gets to broker the sale of an entire insurance company. The kicker is that the state insurance commissioner put Executive Life up for sale in the first place because the company had suffered losses on junk bonds bought from the boys at Drexel Burnham Lambert. That's some solid risk management, and some well-managed cross-selling, indeed.

It's not just the new, integrated financial services companies, like Citigroup and GE Capital, that are placing insurance monies at greater risk. There's a burgeoning market in reinsurance, too. Reinsurance is when insurers sell insurance on insurance to insurers. When your reinsurer has a reinsurer, then that company is called a retrocessionary. Reinsurers don't pay out claims, but they help reimburse the insurance companies that do. As previously noted, the reinsurance industry has been helpful in spreading the costs for September 11 among several concerns, but the fact that more than half the balance is being paid out by reinsurers shows the extent of this business, which most of us know very little about. How easy is it to claim your rightful settlement, when insurers sell part of their risks to other insurers, who sell part of their risk to other insurers—and then they sell it to two friends, and so on, and so on? Reinsurance allows insurance companies to write a greater volume of policy risk than they could otherwise absorb, but that may not be in our best interests, since it means that insurers can go overboard with the underwriting, and may end up playing hot potato, tossing losses to the next insurer, who then passes them to another insurer—and so on and so on.

Even eminently savvy people like Warren Buffett and Saul Steinberg lost bales of spondulicks thanks to a reinsurance tangle involving a pool of workers' comp insurance policies that originated at Unicover, a smallish New Jersey insurer.

They were sold repeatedly, by several major firms to several major firms, apparently before anyone had an idea of exactly how much risk they had taken on. There's a charming name for this practice. It is called "passing the trash." They probably don't call it that when they're selling you a policy, so I doubt you can ask for it by that name. Other dodgy practices by reinsurers have made them part of Spitzer's insurance probe. General Re—the reinsurance wing of Warren Buffett's Berkshire Hathaway group—AIG, and Swiss Re are some of the major reinsurers being questioned about "nontraditional insurance products and certain assumed reinsurance transactions." This is euphemese for "helping our clients cook their books." The attorney general alleges that some transactions that looked like reinsurance or risk-sharing may have been nothing more than sweetheart loan arrangements.

I don't disagree with the concept of insurance. People don't save money, and disease and disaster can strike at any time, so insurance is a necessary evil. However, this necessity is precisely why it is so galling to see insurance monies, private and public, become embroiled in complex, sporadically fraudulent, financial schemes that enrich the fortunate few at the expense of legions of policyholders. Legislation like the Glob channels more insurance money into the wider financial services industry, and Bush's plan to privatize Social Security dispatches public insurance monies in that general direction as well. All the money people think they are salting away for hospital care, fire damage, car wrecks, hurricanes, and old age is sliding further and further into the capable hands of the nice people who brought you corporate scandals and the stock market bust.

Spitzer isn't the only one trying to stick it to the great growing Glob of insurance and banking via the courts. In 2005,

Britney Spears filed suit against her consortium of insurers. They failed to cough up the $9 million she claimed for losses related to a canceled tour. The insurers argued that Britney had failed to disclose that she had a bad knee when she took out the policies. Since the tour was canceled on account of that same blown knee, her claim was rejected. Britney's attorneys argue that the insurers were happy to collect more than a million dollars in premiums from the pop tart, and, like, see ya in court. This case, like insurance itself, leaves me of two minds. It is nice to see insurers reject the long, proud tradition of insuring celebrity body parts and enriching the already rich for spurious losses. It is good to know that there is at least one stalwart sector that remains immune to Spears's dubious charms. On the other hand, Britney filed a claim. Britney lost. Do you have as many lawyers, and as much money, as Britney? If there is no satisfaction for Britney, in the wordy bizarro world of insurance, what chance do we mere mortals have?

CHAPTER EIGHT

MALLS, SPRAWLS, AND TELEPHONE CALLS

Why the Signs Are the Same and the Service Tends to Suck

Who's number one? THE CUSTOMER!
—THE WAL-MART EMPLOYEE CHEER

If you were dropped from the sky on the outskirts of Anytown, North America, it would take you a long time to figure out exactly where you were. There would be plenty of signs, but they wouldn't help much. You would see a big-box store, probably a Wal-Mart or The Home Depot, maybe a mall, with roads and parking in the foreground, and a glass complex or two humming fluorescently in the middle distance. There would probably be three or four kinds of fastfood places close by, but not within walking distance, because nobody walks around these parts. There aren't even sidewalks here. These are the park-and-drive places, twenty to forty minutes from the heart of downtown Wherever. And they are everywhere. The sprawl in Cali may be surrounded by palm trees, and the ones in Quebec may have signs that say *vente* instead of *sale,* but for the most part they are all the same. You got your concrete, you got your offices, you got your hangars

full of merchandise, you got your drive-thru grease kiosks, all
in one convenient traffic snarl.

There are a couple of different factors that helped these
sprawls grow and thrive. The improvement of the highways
opened up more space for urbanized land, and urbanization
has been the trend ever since. Between 1982 and 1997, according to a study on sprawl by the Brookings Institution, the
amount of urbanized land in the United States increased by 47
percent, from about 50 million acres to 76 million. At the same
time, the overall population increased by only 17 percent, and
only a handful of cities became more densely populated. Increasingly, people settled in suburban communities rather
than urban ones. Today, fully half of Americans live in sub-
urbs. There's a correlation between having more space and
buying more stuff: The shopping simply followed the big
houses, aching to be filled with wonderful things, to the cheap
land on the outskirts of town. Shopping used to be an urban
phenomenon, but now it's primarily a sprawl thing. Most
dying downtowns feature the ghostly hulk of a formerly
swanky department store, long since lured to the burbs to an-
chor a mall, or slain by those low, low big-box prices. Environ-
mentalists bemoan this doughnut effect. The city's historic
core rots, leaving pockets of poverty and decrepitude behind.
More outlying fields get paved, pollution spreads, and munici-
palities have to extend the radius of the areas they service.
People end up wasting more time, gas, and money in their
cars, as well.

There are some downtown malls in larger cities, like
Chicago and Boston and Toronto, but the majority are built a
drive away from suburban developments, in the sprawl. The
big-boxes have also helped contribute to, and further accelerate the growth of, sprawl. Since a big-box takes up more than

25,000 square feet, retailers like Wal-Mart and The Home Depot have always gone for the cheapest land they can find, setting up camp at the edge of town. Then all the other businesses, the fast-food joints and plus-size clothing chains and pet care warehouses and electronics stores and Dollaramas and Buck-or-Two junk shops, soon follow, opening strip malls and big-boxes of their own. And so, a hundred thousand sprawls bloom.

Malls and big-boxes are destination shopping, shrines to the boundless bounty of consumer choice. Remember that last long postwar boom, the one where everyone's income went up? With this came a new willingness to buy things just for the hell of it, a desire inflamed by advertisers and the ad-makers' new buddy, television. As theorist William Kowinski put it in his 1985 book, *The Malling of America,* the mall is an extension of your television; it disposes the products and lifestyle the television proposes. This is not even to mention the way that relatively, if regressively, cheap credit has fueled the flames of constant consumption. North Americans are the world's greatest consumers. We can, and will, buy anything. Fifteen years ago, hardly anyone drank bottled water, and today little plastic flasks that read *naive* backwards are as ubiquitous as asphalt. When an oxygen bar opened in Toronto, I didn't know whether to laugh or weep. Part of me thought, silly yuppies, paying for air. The other part of me pictured my future monthly oxygen bill; luxuries have a sneaky way of turning into utilities. The ability to buy whatever you feel like buying has become like a state religion, the very living manifestation of big, beautiful words like *freedom* and *choice.* Shopping isn't just something that we need to do. It's something that most of us want to do.

Shopping isn't just our leisure activity of choice. When the boom went bust and the stock markets were a shambles, who was called on to keep the economy from spiralling into full-blown recession? It wasn't the CEOs, or the government, or even the military, but you, Joe Visa, and you too, Sally Master-Card. Only the consumers could save us now! Zero percent financing and multiple cuts to the interest rate were all attempts to stimulate the mission-critical shopper. Part of the reason why consuming all that can be consumed, like a ravening pack of piranhas, has been elevated to the status of an inalienable right is that the American economy relies heavily on consumer overspending. Previous generations at war have been urged to scrimp and save and have had their food and goods rationed to help the war effort. The avatars of the war on terror urge us to shop till we drop. Changing, or even questioning, our gluttonous binge consumption would mean that—cliché alert—the terrorists have already won. Immediately after September 11, North Americans were told that the best way they could help New York was to go there for dinner and a show and some shopping. While this was, admittedly, a relief effort closer to most people's skill sets than signing up for Doctors Without Borders, it was only what we are usually told to do. Which is, in case you missed the 50 million ads, to spend like a Gabor sister with a fresh husband.

Like every minute of every ad, every inch of retail space entices us to buy more stuff. Between 1970 and 2003, the amount of retail space in the U.S. doubled, and then doubled again, from a billion and a half square feet to 6 billion square feet. I have had the pleasure of being part of the vast mall-o-sphere in my own little way, as a wage slave in a bookstore. You bid adieu to a couple of niceties when you work retail. There are no seats for the serfs. Most retail jobs mean standing all the livelong day, for no reason other than to signal to your customers that you are alert to their every whim. Few are the windows in your average mall. There might be an atrium, but there will be no windows. All that outdoors might distract your eyes from the merch. The mall is climate-controlled, which means it's always the opposite of whatever's happening outside; in the summer, the mall is blissfully cool, and in the winter, it's toasty. It is highly unlikely that you will find a clock, unless it's on sale, because the last thing any store owner or manager wants you to notice is exactly how much time you've spent in the mall. That would totally harsh on your retail mellow. The mall has its own time, promotional time. This is holiday-based, and proceeds seamlessly and ceaselessly from New Year's to Valentine's Day to St. Patrick's Day to Easter to Mother's Day to Memorial Day to Father's Day to Labor Day/Back to School to Halloween to Thanksgiving to Xmas/Hanukkah. This never-ending holiday is part and parcel of the mall's effort to be a fun destination, a place you want to go. But it's a delicate balance; make the mall too comfy-cozy, and freaks who have no intention of buying anything will show up, hang out, and drive the actual shoppers away. If you build a village, even a phony one, eventually, the idiots will come.

In the burbs, malls are pretty much the only place for people to hang out. They are ersatz Main Streets, the gathering places for folks with time on their hands, like seniors and teenagers. Some malls have wholeheartedly embraced the idea of serving as a sort of community center. A few of the earliest mall developments, like Bergen Mall and Garden State Plaza, built in New Jersey in the fifties, included municipal services and meeting rooms for community events. Now that malls are taking it in the face from big-boxes and category killers, many have started renting space out to government and community services, lest they become half-empty dirt malls. But, unlike the town squares of old, or the streets and sidewalks in the city, each and every inch of a mall is privately owned. There have been debates all over North America about whether or not citizens have the right to public assemblies in malls. In the 1980 Supreme Court case of *Pruneyard Shopping Center vs. Robbins,* the justices ruled that it was up to individual states to decide whether malls were the kind of public spaces where people could get their First Amendment on. Some states, like California, Oregon, Massachusetts, and New Jersey, have all recognized malls as a sort of semi-public space, and have protected speech rights in malls.

This is the sort of thing that sends private-property types into conniptions. I think the malls asked for it, with all those walkways and benches and come-hither plastic foliage. But malls only want to be public insofar as you define public as full of people. Besides, these days, hellraisers setting up leaflet tables at the mall is the least of management's worries. I'm sure mall developers fairly long for the days when they had to go to great lengths to keep people out of the mall, now that they face the challenge of getting people to go to the mall at all. About a half billion square feet of the almost 6 billion square feet of retail space in the U.S. is vacant, mainly in dead or dying malls. The new urbanist movement calls them grayfields, and in several states they are trying to refashion them into living communities.

Malls aren't totally dead yet, but they are certainly in decline. The iconic Sherman Oaks Galleria, original home of the eighties Valley Girl, recently closed its doors. Malls have been given a royal beating by a couple of different factors. First of all, micro-malls have leaked into spaces such as offices, airports, and universities. These siphon off some of the burb mall's revenues, but worse still, in making all the world a mall, they make the mall itself less desirable as a place to go. Internet shopping hasn't taken off like the geeks hoped it might, but it's still approximately 44 billion clams that people did not spend at the mall in 2002. The malls that are still very successful, like the West Edmonton Mall and Minnesota's Mall of America, market themselves as destinations.

The biggest enemy of the mall, however, is the new face of retail, the big-box store. Wal-Mart is, of course, the undisputed king of the big-boxes, the grand poobah of the superstores. Wal-Mart is like Mall Lite, all the tasty stuff with less idle meandering. It supplies a wide selection of different goods, just like a mall does, but without the architectural frippery, and for slightly lower prices. Retailing doesn't get much more minimal, ambience-wise, than the Wal-Mart model. Whereas the mall still maintains some semblance of strolling up a street to shop, the big-box store presents you with nothing but the things themselves, in all their cheap profusion. The sheer abundance, if not the quality, of the merch is the star. Each and every Wal-Mart store is simply a giant, fluorescent-lit room, crammed to the unadorned rafters with things, glorious things. Nothing says low, low prices quite like the total absence of decor. No ball room for the kiddies, no coffee for mom, no benches for anyone. Nevertheless, despite the lack of classy blandishments, Wal-Mart is both the number-one retailer and number-one employer in America today. The Walton family has occupied top spots on the annual *Forbes* listing of the richest people in the U.S. since the eighties. In 1979, Wal-Mart finally cleared a billion dollars in sales. By the nineties, they did that much business in a week. In 2003, Wal-Mart's net sales were more than $256 billion. In 2004, they did even better, making $285.2 billion.

Sam Walton, the chain's founder, laid out some of the secrets to his success in his autobiography, *Made in America*. It's a dilly of a read, festooned with fulsome blurbs from Ross Perot, Billy Graham, Bob Hope, and Jack Welch—a helluva barbershop quartet—equating Sam with all that is good and great in the grand U.S. of A. Walton tells the Wal-Mart story from his frantic early days buying and selling bulk cheap wares to his eventual success. His eureka moment came when he was a wholesaler of women's unmentionables. When he tried to sell them for 50 cents, they moved sluggishly. But if he offered three pairs for 99 cents, the panties fairly flew off the shelves. This realization, that lower prices make for greater sales volume, is the cornerstone of the Wal-Mart way. If you make it cheap, people will buy lots more of it, whatever it happens to be.

Sam doesn't list this rule among his top ten tips for building a business. Those are pretty cornpone and commonsensical: Commit to the enterprise and share profits with your partners, Sam's chosen euphemism for his minimum-wage workers. To ward off the specter of unionization, you have to motivate your workers by calling them things like partners or associates, and encourage employee loyalty with rituals like the infamous Wal-Mart cheer. You also have to communicate everything to the partners, blah, blah, blah. While there are a handful of longtime Wal-Mart employees who got in on the ground floor and made a bundle on their stock options, the vast majority of Wal-Mart workers do not participate in the stock option plan. In fact, most of them can't even afford to participate in the health care plan, let alone the investment plan. Most Wal-Mart workers make wages near the legal minimum, and work a full-time week that can be as skimpy as twenty-eight hours. Average U.S. retail wages, which Wal-Mart has helped keep nice and low, are about 200 bucks a week. Way to share.

In a January 2005 article in *The Nation,* writer Liza Feather-stone notes that Wal-Mart got its start in poor communities, has always made most of its money off the poor, and relies on poverty for its continued growth. In an inversion of Henry Ford's policy of paying workers enough to buy his product, Wal-Mart drives wages down so people can afford to shop only at Wal-Mart. Wal-Mart is a notorious union-buster, and made headlines in 2005 for closing a store in Quebec after it went union. No word yet on whether the Quebec workers will sue, but Wal-Mart is among the most sued entities in the world. Several of these suits involve labor law infractions, like making people work off the clock, or allegations of discrimination against the women and minorities that make up the bulk of the Wal-Mart associate force. In June of 2004, courts certified the largest civil-rights class action suit in the U.S. system, *Dukes vs. Wal-Mart,* which alleges that the retailer systematically underpaid and underpromoted over a million female workers. Wal-Mart is still appealing the decision.

Sam makes his business sound customer-centric and employee-friendly. And though Walton was a union-buster, it seems that the old duffer really did make nice with his partners on his frequent visits to Wal-Mart stores. Since Sam's death in 1992, though, the Son of Sam Wal-Mart has become increasingly ruthless with its suppliers, employees, and competitors. The Wal-Mart way goes a little something like this. Squeeze your suppliers for their lowest prices, and then underprice all the local competition. Once everyone else goes out of business, raise your prices. Simple as a dimple, ain't it? The fancy antitrust law name for this sort of thing is predatory pricing. One study by an Iowa economist estimated that when Wal-Mart came to the state, Iowa lost half of its clothing stores, 40 percent of its variety stores, 25 percent of its department stores, and 30 percent of its hardware stores. Another study by a New York state advocacy group estimated that for every lousy job a Wal-Mart created, one and a half local jobs were lost. Other retailers can try to compete with Wal-Mart, but they usually do so by specializing and gentrifying. This is why you can buy any number of charming tchtochkes and upscale wares from specialized retailers downtown, but you can't find basic household goods like a mop or dishes or sheets to save your life. The only place you can get that kind of stuff is a big-box, or the mall.

As for all that "Made in America" flag-waving, most Wal-Mart products aren't. Remember Kathie Lee, mascara-smeared and penitent, when she discovered her awful leisure wear was lovingly stitched by underpaid foreign children? Those togs were on sale at Wal-Mart, and they're still shilling the best glad rags that sweatshops have to offer. Wal-Mart is one of the largest importers of sweatshop products from Central America and Asia. Wal-Mart imported $15 billion worth of merchandise from China alone in 2004, comprising more than 10 percent of the U.S. trade deficit with China. Wal-Mart has also been ordering suppliers with manufacturing operations based in more expensive locales to relocate to China, if they wish to continue doing business with the company.

Wal-Mart's latest move is into the grocery industry, as their new Superstores feature a full grocery store, nestled among all the other merchandise. These Superstores have made Wal-Mart America's biggest grocer, and its third biggest pharmacy. Grocery employee unions have been howling about how the incursion of the big-boxes is closing down regional chains and making their living-wage jobs a thing of the past. Wal-Mart's move into the grocery industry has already destroyed dozens of midsized regional supermarket chains. Wal-Mart is also considering used-car dealerships in their parking lots. It's not enough that they sell a goodly chunk of America's household goods. They want to sell you your food as well, and the car you use to drive the lot home. They've also started filing applications to get involved in the financial services industry. Some Wal-Marts carry money orders, and they are itching to get their hands on your mortgage, too. Just imagine the Wal-Mart of the glorious future: you can work there, bank there, and buy everything you need there. Hooray, one-stop shopping! Just like the Company Store! It's sooo convenient.

Walton urges businessmen to think small, which hardly sounds convincing coming from a man who started a very big chain of very big stores. But it's true. You can chuckle at the cheerleading and the greeters, but that little shred of Ma and Pa Kettle–style retailing that Wal-Mart clings to, for all its technological advancement and enormousness, is one of the reasons why it is such a success. Why, y'aren't standin' in a detachment of the world's most voracious retail behemoth! No, this is your community store. The key is to fake small, to try to make every interaction with the customer seem cozy and personal. Wal-Mart's ad campaigns feature "local" folks, from wherever the ads air. Some of these just plain folks are Wal-Mart employees, and others are satisfied customers, but they are always doing something perfectly ordinary: A middle-aged couple gardens, a couple of college gals spruce up their dorm room, a family gets ready for their new baby, all with Wal-Mart's invaluable aid. This is cheaper than hiring some big-name celebrity, and it also strikes the appropriate folksy, local note. There are a million different cheesy motivational manuals about customer service, but success ultimately comes down to creating the illusion that the transaction is all about you.

Through copious lashings of advertising, and by training employees to kiss every ass that comes through the door, stores endeavor to convince you that every rinky-dink chunk of mass-produced bric-a-brac was manufactured expressly for you, the almighty customer.

The Wal-Mart smocks used to read, "Our people make the difference," in keeping with Sam's boosterish employee relations style. Now they read, "How may I help you?," which may well be, and I type this heaving a sigh, the most oft-repeated question of our time. It's certainly way ahead of "To be, or not to be?" And the world would be the portrait of Christian charity if people meant help like actual help whenever they said it, but the phrase actually means something more like "May I fetch you another product or service, my liege?" Because, see, it's all about you, you customer you. The elastic-waist slacks are for you, the pills are for you, the patio furniture is for you, wonderful you.

The retail and service sectors have to make it seem like it is all about you to get your business, but getting your business is all about them. For all the small talk, at the new Son of Sam Wal-Mart, the goal is bigger, faster, and more. They used to open a store every couple of days. Now they're trying to do one a day, all over the world. They've been putting them up in Europe and Latin America, and are also wooing that awakening Chinese market, a drool-inducing prospect for any merchandiser . . . mmmm, billions of big-box virgins, who have never known the full flower of Western retail . . . mmmm. All the big stores, all the category killers, work the same way. They're fiercely competitive—within themselves. Wal-Mart, Starbucks, and The Home Depot routinely open branches within a few miles or meters of each other and let them sell each other to the death. Once they destroy the local competition by saturating the market, and identify which of their own outlets has the best turnover, they close the less successful outlets and redirect the traffic to the winning stores.

Walton dismissed the claim that his chain has slaughtered small-town Ma and Pa Kettle retailers, and guffawed at the notion that they should be protected, like endangered whooping cranes. Sam preferred to highlight the billions he's saved Americans by offering low, low prices. I love the way he, and all Wal-Mart's defenders, deploy this savings argument—by spending billions of dollars at Wal-Mart, you've actually conserved billions. The only problem with this kind of feel-good math is that the only saved billions in evidence are those in the Wal-Mart bank accounts. You simply cannot save more money by buying lots of things, even if you're buying cheaper things. Even though Wal-Mart is praised by free-marketeers for bringing down the price of household goods, those low, low prices have only encouraged people to buy more shit. Wal-Mart is an expert in the art of impulse merchandising. You go in for a mop, and you leave with a bunch of other stuff, because it's all right there. The effectiveness of this particular savings plan is clear; most households are, if not drowning, at least wallowing in consumer debt, and the savings rate remains negative. If folks are saving a couple of bucks on their mops and what-not, they are certainly not banking any of those gains, unlike the billion-stashing beast of Bentonville.

It's not just that we're stark-raving shopaholics, though we most certainly are. Nor is it simply that we are buying more of our goods from large, distant concerns that do jack for our local economies. Fast-food outlets and big-box stores act as a drag on revenues for most cities and municipal regions since they entail road and service costs and contribute little to the tax base. In fact, a Democratic staff report for the U.S. House

Committee on Education and the Workforce estimates that a Wal-Mart store with two hundred staffers ends up costing the government more than $400,000 in low-income tax credits and health and housing subsidies. Way to externalize. The really swell news about the new service economy is that serving and waiting are what most of us will be doing for a living. The service industry and retail sales, both denizens of the sprawl, are two of the biggest employers in the United States, and will continue to lead job growth for the next decade or so.

The service industry, which includes everything from restaurant and motel workers to health care helpers and janitors, is the fastest-growing sector, and should continue to lead job growth until 2010, according to the National Bureau of Labor Statistics. The Bureau puts together a report called the Occupational Outlook Handbook, which goes by the delightful acronym of OOH, where they predict what jobs will be big over the next decade. And in keeping with that whole increasing economic inequality thing, there are two trends at work. There will be a greater demand for professional and managerial types. As the boomers age and retire, new suits will be needed to fill the ranks, and we'll need heaps of teachers and nurses too. But the greatest job growth will be on the plains of service, not in the citadels of management. The top ten jobs for the next decade are:

1. Combined food preparation and service, including fast food
2. Customer service representatives
3. Registered nurses
4. Retail salespersons
5. Computer support specialists
6. Cashiers, except gaming

7. Office clerks, general
8. Security guards
9. Computer software engineers
10. Waiters and waitresses

OOH, indeed. This is a list you should show the kids. Might as well break it to them sooner, rather than later. And what would you like to be when you grow up, Timmy? An astronaut? Silly Timmy! Why, there are only a couple of hundred astronauts in the whole wide world, little guy. Be realistic. Why not try a rewarding career as a customer service representative, inbound calls only? Beats hell out of steaming in grease at Mickey D's!

The only gigs on that list that pay worth a damn are the two computer things and the nursing gig. The service industry does offer a slightly better rate of pay than the retail average of just above minimum wage, but this depends on what type of service you perform. Some service jobs are unionized, and the Service Employees International Union, which has 1.8 million members in the U.S., Canada, and Puerto Rico, is one of the fastest-growing labor organizations in America. However, most of the workers in the retail trade and service industries are not unionized. And those cushy computer jobs are the latest to be outsourced to cheaper foreign workers, which is driving the wages of geekdom down. The vast majority of people who work in fields like retail and food service make wages near the legal minimum.

I am quite sure that you have a good idea of what services fast-food workers perform—the frying, the nuking, the smiling. You may have even worn the ceremonial smock and hairnet yourself at one point or another. The customer service representative, number two on the OOH, is a slightly more enigmatic creature. Customer service representative is a catch-all term that encompasses service over the Internet and phone. There are more than 50,000 call centers in America, and they employ about 3 million people. Those are necessarily rough estimates, as call centers tend to experience very high levels of employee turnover. The average employment stint at a call center is a year and a half. This is doubtless due to the fact that call center jobs, for all that they may have a sheen of white-collar office gentility, are usually stressful and boring.

There are two different branches of call center work, the outbound and the inbound. Inbound calls only, a real selling point in call center classifieds, means that you will only have to take calls from customers who want to hear from you. Outbound means sales, or telemarketing, which means getting hung up on and berated. Be they inbound or outbound, most call centers are simply phone-answering factories, hotbeds of psycho-Taylorist efficiency. Employees usually work in one large space, headsetted before their pods, cubicled a few feet away from each other. A fascinating article in *Call Center Magazine* enthuses about the fact that you can pack twice as many workers into a call center space than into a traditional office. In a regular office, zoning laws insist that you need to have 1,000 square feet for every four people, but in a call center you can cram eight phone jockeys in the same amount of space. In a pleasant bit of new economy synergy, the article also recommends decommissioned Wal-Marts—there are hundreds to choose from—as an excellent, economical venue for your call center.

The biggest problem with the way call centers are currently run is that performance tends to be measured by quantity, rather than quality. Call turnover is a lot easier to track than customer satisfaction. While supervisors are encouraged to listen in on calls, and most recordings warn that your call may be monitored for quality control, it is far easier to judge CSRs on speed than on the finer points of service. The more calls CSRs take, and the quicker they take them, the better they do. Even in call centers that involve service rather than sales, workers may be required to fill call quotas, or stick to scripts, and are discouraged from tarrying with any one customer. Consequently, the employee who dispatches with several complaints quickly by failing to fix or know anything actually performs better than the employee who takes the time to investigate your problem.

I did an unscientific poll of my own and asked a friend who works for a bank call center to count how many calls he took during an eight-hour shift. He took eighty-seven calls that shift and described the day as not particularly busy, just steady, and eighty calls per shift often comes up as a sort of call center industry standard. A busy day would be more like twenty calls an hour. All the whip-cracking and chop-chop is because employee time is money. One way to cut these labor costs is to hire people in other regions where labor is cheaper—like jail. Prisons are good sites for your call center. UNICOR, otherwise known as Federal Prison Industries, calls itself "the best-kept secret in outsourcing," noting that prison labor rates are competitive with offshore hubs like India, and that prisoners have the added advantage of familiar accents. However, there have been some concerns about allowing convicted felons to get their hands on data like phone and credit card numbers, so even companies like TWA that use prison labor to staff call centers tend not to brag about it.

Down-on-their-luck Canadian provinces are also excellent sites for your call center. The favorable exchange rate is part of the charm, as are the tax incentives from cash-strapped local governments. Nova Scotia and New Brunswick have been wooing call centers as a way of boosting employment rates, and there are some big cubicle farms out in the Halifax sprawl, where pals of mine take office supply orders from bored Pentagon secretaries and try to straighten out erroneous cell phone charges for irate Texans. Maritimers are polite, friendly, and poor, and the fact that the government picks up the tab for health insurance attracts plenty of American companies, such as Xerox, to our fair shores.

Nova Scotia's governments have sold call center jobs as an alternative to lost jobs in fishing and manufacturing. The province claims that the payroll tax incentives they offer are worthwhile, if they can lure the kind of jobs that pay about 10 clams an hour, and provide some benefits. However, some outfits have only lasted as long as the incentives have. A Sears catalog outlet lasted barely a year, despite six-figure subsidies. Moreover, as the Canadian dollar climbs, the Great White North becomes less competitive, wage-wise, making Nova Scotia but one stop on a race to the bottom of the labor-costs barrel. India is an increasingly popular call center outsource; their English is pretty good, and they work for four times less money than their North American coevals.

Of course, the only thing cheaper than brown people is robots. This is why the ATM is everywhere and bank teller is just about the only service job in decline. If a website or workbot can do the job, and serve us without seeing us or speaking to us, then the company saves a bundle. Most big companies have set up websites, in the hope that we'll do everything online, or on the phone. Some companies have set up genuinely helpful sites; others have erected cordons sanitaires. Your call, whether it's to your bank, phone company, cable company, or airline, hardly ever goes straight to a person. I'm downright discombobulated nowadays when I call a company and don't get the dulcet tones of that voice-mail woman, the Lady Hal. The Lady Hal greets you with a menu of prompts, each one a different route for your call. This is important, because Repairs may be outsourced to a different center than Billing. You are also encouraged to punch in the strings of digits that attach themselves, lamprey-like, to any and all transactions. This is so your information will "pop up" on the employee's computer when the CSR finally takes your call. Some companies allow you to fill prescriptions, or do some banking, by simply punching in the appropriate numbers. A call that stays in the voice-mail system costs the company only pennies; a call between people costs dollars. This is one of the reasons why IVR, otherwise known as Interactive Voice Response, is the talk of the call center industry. Instead of punching in your numbers, and waiting on hold for a rep, the whole transaction is gloriously person-free. You'll simply tell the Lady Hal exactly what to do.

Of course, many of us have already told her exactly what to do, and where to go, while languishing for seemingly interminable periods listening to lickspittle from the Lady Hal. If I had a nickel for every time I've heard her intone the phrases, "We are experiencing higher than usual call volumes," "Your call will be answered in priority sequence," and the Big Lie, "Your call is important to us," I wouldn't be writing this book. I'd be charging admission and selling snacks at my fabulous roadside attraction, Nickel Mountain. When you are waiting on hold, all the things you have been promised as a customer go out the window. You are not always right, and you are no king. You are just another cluster of digits in the priority sequence.

The factory-floor model of labor, where unskilled persons

perform repetitive tasks repeatedly, works fine if you're drilling some holes or welding a chassis. It does not work so well when the task is to explain to a consumer why their computer is having seizures, or to track a series of payments through a digital labyrinth. Your bank, or airline, or cable company provides a complex array of services, each with its own set of codes and prohibitions and prices, all stored on legions of computers, manned by many fallible individuals. A million things can go wrong, and they do. But when you try to rectify your problems, insult is added to injury. Most businesses do not hire enough front-line customer service personnel, so you have to suffer infuriating wait times. Then, once you finally get to speak to someone, he or she simply does not have the expertise, or the incentive, or the authority to fix your problem. Should your request be beyond the bounds of the CSR's limited powers, the next step is to transfer you to another department, which may be in an entirely different call center, and may involve waiting in another priority sequence. Or, your CSR can call for a supervisor. In call center lingo, they call the call for a supervisor "escalation." Escalation is discouraged, since there are generally far fewer supervisors than there are employees. Industry figures put the ratio at about ten employees per supervisor, but my anecdotal survey suggests this is a generous estimate. This is why, when you ask an unhelpful employee to transfer you to a supervisor, you go back into the holding pattern for a while. And even though you can't hear them, behind the wall of Muzak and the stylings of the Lady Hal, they can always hear you, swearing and sputtering.

Call centers don't have to be voice-mail hells. There are some that boast high customer satisfaction ratings, and they share a few common traits, all of which make perfect sense. First, good call centers spend time training their people, so they are informed about the services their companies provide. Second, they hire more personnel, which cuts down on annoying wait times and encourages workers to spend more time with each customer. Third, they pay their workers better and offer opportunities for promotion. But all this costs money that companies would prefer to spend elsewhere, like on their advertising, say.

This is another of the problems with service today, the great honking oversell of advertising. A doctrine that decrees that one is always right is a doctrine that is bound to disappoint. Companies pitch some serious woo when they're trying to build a relationship with you. Throughout the balmy boom, companies promised us the moon. The new technology was going to make every transaction as easy as clicking a mouse, or phoning it in. Unfortunately, the technology still needs lots of people to run it, labor that big companies are not willing to pay for. Throughout the nineties, despite all the technological improvements in the service industry, customer satisfaction fell. According to the American Consumer Satisfaction Index, a study conducted by the University of Michigan, it slid downhill from 1994, when the survey started, till 1998. Customer satisfaction levels bounced up and down around the turn of the millennium, but then September 11 made shopping a patriotic imperative and the scores rose, borne aloft by zero percent financing. However, the most recent estimates from the ACSI, for the last quarter of 2004, show customer satisfaction levels at a record low, dropping to a score of 73.6 out of 100.

This wasn't a huge decline. Customer satisfaction scores have been around 75 points for the duration of the study. That's only a C. And this study is funded by the industries it analyzes, so one would expect it to skew in their favor. Moreover, some behemoths didn't do nearly as well as you might

expect them to do. Wal-Mart's been on the slippity-slide since
the survey started, from a score of 80 in 1994 to their latest
score, 70, for the fourth quarter of 2004. McDonald's scored a
63 in 1994, and it has bounced around the low sixties and high
fifties ever since. The most recent quarterly figures, from 2003,
put Mickey D's at 64, comparable to the hated airlines. People
don't go to these places for the service. What kind of service do
McDonald's employees or Wal-Mart workers perform? It's
pretty much the bare minimum. They heat stuff up and hand
it to you, or they get things off the shelf and ring them in. The
best-ranked company on the survey, with a score of 84, was
e-tailer Amazon.com, a company where all the workers are
totally invisible. You simply serve yourself online, in the
comfort of your home, and the products just show up at your
door. Poof! No interactions with fumbling, diffident employees, just a hit of straight-up commerce, quick and sure and
pure.

The computer has allowed companies like Amazon to cus-
tomize customer service, but not always in a good way. In
keeping with the old business chestnut that 80 percent of the
profits come from 20 percent of the customers, service is becoming increasingly stratified according to income. Better
data collection means that companies are better able to engage
in financial profiling. Computers make it easier for companies
to figure out exactly how much it costs them to help you, and
exactly how much your business is worth to them. As an article
in *BusinessWeek* put it, a tad melodramatically, "Welcome to
the new consumer apartheid." One bank grades all its customers with a color code that pops up whenever they call;
greens are the big spenders, reds the losers, and yellows the in-
betweeners. The CSRs tailor the transaction accordingly. If
you're poor, you can expect the same serve-yourself model

that prevails at Wal-Mart. If you're a high roller, you can expect premium service: *Your* call is important to them.

We may kvetch about the decline of old-school, hands-on, informed service, but when we shop, we consistently opt for the quick and the cheap. Consequently, most service sucks because serving people sucks. Why do a good job if you don't have a good job? The top ten jobs are the top ten jobs in part because most of them have high turnover rates; they're gigs that people leave in months, not years. Most people drift from call centers to big-boxes to fast-food joints. They feel no loyalty to or compunctions about their ginormous, distant employers, and it shows. Even Henry Ford figured out that you had to pay your workers enough to afford the things they produced in order to run a sustainable business, a lesson lost on most service and retail employers. And yet, in spite of all these glum stats about poorly paid workers delivering C-level service, and households maintaining their right to buy via mounting debt loads, free-marketeers insist that this is the system that works, the one thing that satisfies our wants and needs. The market isn't just the best economic system, though it's certainly that, by leaps and bounds, like a Porsche is better than a splintery old oxcart. No, marketeers go on and on and on as if all this buying and selling is the sole feat of human organization functioning as it should, and use the market as the benchmark for other services, like government, schools, and hospitals. You are no longer a citizen, a student, or a patient; you're a customer. Hooray, everyone is number one! What a load of steaming number two.

CHAPTER NINE

SLEAZE BITES AND FLUFF CRAWLS

or Can We Dumb This Down for the Kids?

Freedom of the press is limited to those who own one.

—A.J. LIEBLING

I am a news junkie. When I was young, I dreamed of being a dashing, righteous foreign correspondent, à la Christiane Amanpour. I imagined speaking truth to power from war-torn wherever. I even enrolled in journalism school. After a term, I realized I hated interviewing people. I didn't like writing in industry-standard inverted pyramids. I didn't like leaving the house, let alone jetting off to still-sizzling, recently wrecked locales. I excelled at lying on my couch in my pajamas reading long, boring things and writing short, amusing things, so I changed majors, and became a professional nerd. But I never lost J-school habits like reading a couple of papers and watching the news every day. Newspapers, magazines, radio, television, and the Internet have brought me hours—nay, years—of wonkish pleasure. Consequently, it pains me to take my beloved free press to task. But I chide and chastise because I care, and because the media are such an important part of the bullshit pandemic. The media are a critical line of defense against, and a great disseminator of, bullshit. They have the power to make shit up, let shit slide, or make sure that the shit hits the fan.

A variety of vocal constituencies think that the Main Stream Media (MSM) are full of shit. Right-wingers accuse the media of liberal bias. Liberals accuse the media of being shills for Bush and big business. Old-school, retired journalists have written a number of books arguing that the profession is in dire straits. A number of scandals, in particular the Stephen Glass and Jayson Blair imbroglios, gave the media the opportunity to hate the media, and engage in many column inches of anxious self-examination. Bloggers of both political persuasions have debunked or scooped MSM stories, and have made incursions into MSM domains like political conventions. Hell, even the president disdains the media. When a reporter asked Bush which news outlets he preferred, he replied that he didn't really care for any of them. He doesn't bother with the distortions of the press. He has people he trusts to tell him what is going on.

Even people who are in the news every day can't be arsed with the news anymore.

Public trust in the media has been declining for the past twenty years, according to the Project for Excellence in Journalism. Their 2004 report on the state of American journalism is full of grim stats. Only 49 percent of the respondents in their study thought the press was professional, down from 72 percent in 1985. And 36 percent thought the press was actively immoral, while 67 percent thought the press try to cover up their mistakes. Twenty years ago, 55 percent figured the press had their facts straight; now only 35 percent believe this.

There was, however, a brief period within recent memory when these trends reversed, and the public trusted the press

again, if only for a couple of months. After September 11, ratings for the news and approval ratings for the media soared. The
disaster inspired many in the media to declare the end of the
rule of the frivolous and the scandalous. Before September 11,
the media spent the summer gabbing about Gary Condit and
sharks. After September 11, the Gary Condit story became the
standard example of the kind of sensationalistic, tawdry tale
that the media would no longer stoop to tell. Media culpa,
media culpa, media maxima culpa, cried the press corps, beating their breasts and packing their bags for some old-school
front-line reportage, live from foreign hellholes. From here on
in, it was just the facts, ma'am. No more sleaze and fluff, like
Condit and sharks. We were going to get real news, war news,
hard news.

Hard news is news about public policy issues and foreign
affairs, and it's the kind of news that has been on the wane lo
these past twenty years. In the seventies, foreign affairs coverage made up about 45 percent of TV news. As of 1995, that was
down to a trifling 14 percent. Even during January 2002, when
the War on Terror was shifting from Afghanistan to Iraq, foreign affairs coverage only made up about 21 percent of the
nightly news, and less than 1 percent of the morning news.
Moreover, that coverage tended to be disaster coverage, simply
delivering the death tolls for the latest Israeli/Palestinian skir-
mish or Third World famine, earthquake, or drought, rather
than explaining what was up with the rest of the world. By
2002, people had drifted away from coverage of international
events, since they lacked the background to understand the
stories, felt they were too far away to be relevant to them, or
had tired of talk of war and violence.

News outlets, from broadcasts to broadsheets, have increasingly favored soft news over hard news. Soft news is all that

fluff that has nothing to do with foreign affairs or public policy. Celebrity reportage, human interest profiles, and scandal reporting have ballooned and floated from gossip columns to the news proper. Crime reporting has more than doubled since the eighties, even though the overall crime rate has steadily declined. The time devoted to human interest stories, and the lifestyle and consumer reporting that falls under the category of "news you can use," has also more than doubled. The vocabulary of journalism has changed, too, with a shift in emphasis from the collective nouns of hard news to increased usage of personal pronouns.

At the same time that the coverage has skewed from hard to soft, the way people get their news has changed as well. Broadcast journalism has continued to trounce the grimy old newspaper as most people's primary source of information. Only 42 percent of the Americans who follow the news do so by reading a paper. Almost twice as many people, 83 percent, watch TV news. But broadcast news has changed, too. It is no longer the exclusive province of the stodgy old nightly newscasts on the big three U.S. networks. CNN, founded in 1980, inaugurated a whole spectrum of cable news networks, providing round-the-clock coverage. According to a survey by the Pew Research Center for the People and the Press, a decade ago 60 percent of viewers used to tune in to one of the big three nightly newscasts. Now less than a third of the audience gets their news from CBS, ABC, and NBC. Cable news claims a third of the audience, and most of those people are watching CNN or Fox News, which are locked in a bitter struggle for ratings supremacy. I will get to this battle of the 24–7 news titans in a few pages, but first, let's look at why the news has gotten all squidgy on us.

Hard news isn't cheap. It's much less expensive to cover the latest Beltway indignity or Hollywood murder than it is to schlep a crew to war-torn wherever, or fund a time-consuming, potentially litigation-inducing series of investigative reports. The switch to soft news is also an attempt to improve ratings and please advertisers. This drive to cut costs while improving ratings is a significant shift in the way networks think about the news. In the heyday of the big three, the nightly news was seen as a sort of public service. ABC, CBS, and NBC have never been charities, but they saw their nightly newscasts as an obligation, a way of saying thanks for all the free airwaves granted to them by the FCC. Legendary CBS chief William Paley told his news division not to worry about making money. That wasn't their job. They had stars like Jack Benny to make the money.

Today the news is a moneymaking enterprise, a product that, like all the others, is expected to produce perpetual profit. The news has become just another part of the wonderful world of content. Content is the buzzword for all the media products people consume, from blockbuster movies to best-selling books to hit singles to Web portals to your news. The term *content provider* was originally an Internet term, but now everyone from the aged hosts of *60 Minutes* to the latest pre-pubescent novelty rapper is a content provider. And the term *content* has become popular because media companies have become more consolidated, with fewer players selling more entertainment, information, and infotainment, and, let us not forget, copious quantities of advertainment. The only way to explain those madly diversified holdings is to lump 'em all under a term like *content,* as though books and music and news and movies were of a piece, information units to be marketed and moved.

In 1984, there were more than fifty companies in the U.S. that held a controlling interest in newspapers, radio stations, TV stations, and book and magazine publishers. By 2002, that number was down to less than a dozen. Media theorist Ben Bagdikian estimates that the number of companies controlling the global media is somewhere between twenty and six, the big six being AOL Time Warner, Bertelsmann, News Corp, Vivendi, Viacom, and Disney. If I wanted to bulk up my relatively modest volume, and make it nice and hefty like an edition of Proust, I could spend pages galore just listing the media products produced by these six companies. The big six own pretty much every set of letters in the alphabet soup of broadcasting, like CNN, TBS, WB, AOL, BMG, RCA, FOX, MTV, CBS, and ABC, to name but a few. Suffice it to say that if you live on this planet, and have ever turned on your TV, read a magazine or book, or enjoyed pop culture in any form whatsoever, you have beheld the mighty works of the big six. Six! Their respective CEOs could hold an evil cabal in the cozy confines of a minivan.

We may have more channels than ever before, but centralized ownership, by a handful of companies, means more of what they like to call synergy and cross-promotion. And more synergy and cross-promotion means samey-style blobbiness, entertainment in your news, and news in your entertainment. Screwy bran-and-jujubes combinations ensue, and the next thing you know, a divertissement like *Survivor* turns up on the morning news and in the paper. And then blockbuster schlockmeister Jerry Bruckheimer starts talking to ABC about producing a mini-series about the War on Terror. Or you get absurdities like *Saving Private Jessica,* the movie, like the news story wasn't a movie to begin with. The news has become more like entertainment, with fast editing, flashier graphics, and prettier people. Meanwhile, entertainment wraps itself in the gravitas of news. Box-office totals for weekend movie openings are now a standard news item. Every major network has at least one prime-time newsmagazine, which features extended coverage of gruesome crimes or amazing trials, intimate chinwags with the stars, and exposés of the horrors lurking in your own home, alarmist shit like "Bath Towels: The Fluffy Killer!" Then there are all those shows like *Entertainment Tonight* and *Extra,* the news' dimwitted, hyper little sisters, squealing at shiny people. *ET* was a flop at first, until a passing news director told the producers to sell it as news. Didn't matter if it was just publicity—which is all celeb coverage is—so long as it looked like news. *20/20* suffered from similar wobbly ratings early on, until an ABC vice president offered the one-word suggestion that saved the fledgling newsmagazine: *entertainment.*

One of the most frequently invoked reasons for the increase in sensationalistic semi-news is that the media marketplace is simply giving the people what they want. People aren't interested in the tedious intricacies of the new farm bill. That stuff is seriously snore-making. The people want sex and violence and scandals and scares. The people want live coverage of car chases. That's what gets the ratings, not blah-dee-blah about policy or lengthy expostulations about unstable foreign countries. Or so they tell us. But when we viewers are asked what we want in our news, without fail we value things like timeliness and accuracy over entertainment value and attractive talking heads. Soft news isn't entertaining enough to lure viewers away from entertainment programming, but it's fluffy enough to piss off the folks who like a little news in their news. Contrary to the corporate catechism that the dumber, lighter, and flashier stories always mean better ratings, there is a market for hard news.

In the first few months after September 11, hard news made a roaring comeback, comprising 80 percent of U.S. television reportage. The media didn't just talk more about what happened yesterday, they started to talk about why it happened. They also reinvested in foreign bureaus, used more sources, and named their sources more frequently. Even the morning shows, which were basically product-pushing lifestyle infomercials before September 11, started devoting more than half their segments to hard news. The result? Ratings for the news and the press in general improved appreciably, after years of steady decline. People watched the news, talked about the news, and read books to learn more about the things they heard about on the news. Sure, some of that interest was fueled by terror. But it was fed and sustained by reporting, until the Bush administration clammed up and clamped down, and the networks realized they were spending way too much money.

After a few months of enthusiasm and effort, viewers started to get tired of the complexities of hard news. Two decades of increasing fluffiness meant that it was awfully difficult for the audience to get up to speed on their -stans, and the other fine points of international affairs. As the *Onion* headline put it, a shattered nation longed to care about stupid bullshit again. The public trust that the media had gained in the months after September 11 leaked away, and returned to pre-9–11 levels, in less than a year. Once Afghanistan was in the can, bullshit stories, stuff like the Robert Blake trial and the Elizabeth Smart kidnapping, came crawling back to their customary omnipresence. Kidnapped kids were the mainstay of

Connie Chung's much-hyped show on CNN, which also featured occasional palate-cleansing forays into frivolous litigation. Chung's show was one of the first victims of the War in Iraq, postponed and then canceled to make way for constant coverage. However, even constant war coverage didn't totally preempt the Laci Peterson mini-series, which was a little bit Court TV, a little bit Lifetime, and a sneaky way to advance the pro-life cause of fetal rights as well, via Laci and Connor's Law.

The war in Iraq has been the lead story in the news for the past couple of years. When major combat operations began, the administration came up with a wonderful way of accommodating the public's desire to know, and aiding and abetting their friends in the press. Enter the "embedded reporter," which, as many folks have noted, sounds an awful lot like "in bed with." Embedded journalists traveled alongside the troops in the Persian Gulf. While this might seem like an unprecedented level of openness and access, what this really meant was that the military controlled every aspect of embedded reportage. Many of the justifications the administration offered for the war, like Iraq's ties to terrorism, or possession of weapons of mass destruction, have since been proven utterly bogus by the media. But the Bush administration greets every criticism with the same deflecting defense: We must move on in the war against terror, we must never forget 9–11, we must punish the evildoers, we must spread freedom and democracy, may God continue to bless America. When journalists have the temerity to pick at the propaganda and platitudes in search of the facts, they usually find themselves deflected on the grounds of national security and classified information. If they keep it up, and run stories critical of the administration, they find themselves exiled to source Siberia, denied access to information and interviews on account of their nitpicking. The "you're with us or against us" rhetoric of war and foreign affairs also extends to the media.

The Bush administration may well be the most secretive, press-repelling one since Nixon. In his first term, despite presiding over a national crisis, a recession, and steady warfare, Bush held fewer solo press conferences than any modern president. Bush did eleven press conferences, and only three of them aired during prime time. Eleven! Clinton held thirty-eight press conferences over the course of his first term. Bush the Elder, though he may have been the grand poobah of the sentence fragment, spoke to the press seventy-one times. Dubya is not a big fan of taking questions from the press, and it shows. He becomes visibly surly when the media tries to drag him off-message. In the April 13, 2004, press conference, one of the prime-time ones, Bush got rattled when a reporter asked him about his mistakes. What did the president think his biggest mistake was? Had he learned from his mistakes? The president bristled and said: "I wish you would have given me this written question ahead of time, so I could plan for it. John, I'm sure historians will look back and say, gosh, he could have done it better this way, or that way. You know, I just—I'm sure something will pop into my head here in the midst of this press conference, with all the pressure of trying to come up with an answer, but it hadn't (sic) yet."

Bush went on to state that he was confident weapons would be found, and that Saddam was a dangerous man. He was flustered, but back on book. Then he remembered the impertinent query, and he said he was confident he had made mistakes, but couldn't think of any, what with being put on the spot and all.

Put on the spot? When you're the president, you *live* on the spot. I wish this book could include a video clip, because the transcript and the description don't really do this exchange justice. You need to see the video to catch all the dead air, the fumbling, and the frustrated hemming and hawing. It also helps to hear Bush's sarcastic, affronted tone as he blusters his way through his nonanswer. What really surprised me about this question was that it seemed to totally blindside the president: Dubya and his handlers didn't even plan a joke response to the question about mistakes, something like, "Well, Laura's been keeping me off the pretzels," har-dee-har-har.

The administration shuns direct questioning by the press, and prefers staging little tableaux vivants, like the "Mission Accomplished" landing on the aircraft carrier, or prepared orations, like the State of the Union and his speeches before vetted crowds. The Republicans have also created their very own media to combat and infiltrate the MSM. Karl Rove got his start in direct mail, and the Republicans still use it at as a right-wing samizdat, a way of spreading stories unfit to print. As previously noted in the PR chapter, the Republicans have paid pundits to praise their initiatives and distributed video news releases to television stations. In February 2005, bloggers broke the story of Jeff Gannon, a White House correspondent for an organization called Talon News. Jeff was a regular at White House press briefings from 2003 until 2005, when the blogosphere began wondering who this guy was and how the hell he got a White House press pass. They discovered the following: Talon News is a fake news front for GOPUSA, a Republican group run by a Texan named Bernard Eberle, who has long supported Bush and Rove. Jeff Gannon had no prior reporting experience or credentials, save for a two-day workshop at a right-wing think tank. Jeff's questions and articles reproduced, verbatim, talking points from the administration. Jeff Gannon is not even his real name. It may be James D.

Guckert, and it may be something else, but it ain't Jeff Gannon. Gannon's career previous to his time in the press corps? Personal trainer and gay male escort. Nobody has explained why Gannon kept getting daily press passes for years when a number of legitimate media outlets would kill to get that kind of access. Nor has anyone explained how a guy with a fake name gets past all that post 9–11 security.

People like Gannon are part of the network of right-wing think tanks and front groups and professional bloviators that has helped move public discourse rightward and selfward over the past twenty years. But the right also has its very own cable network, Fox News. I write this chapter at an unfortunate distance from the mother lode: I don't get Fox News. The CRTC, Canada's FCC, finally approved Fox News's application to broadcast on digital cable in 2004. John Doyle, a television columnist for the *Globe and Mail,* wrote that he couldn't wait for the channel to come to Canada. He saw it in the States and thought it was a riot, and figured the rest of us would find it pretty hilarious, too. This bit of impunity landed him on Fox News and right-wing message boards, and he got hundreds of hate e-mails denouncing him, his socialist paper, and his communist country. The few choice snippets of Fox News I have seen on Canadian television have largely been from Fox News reports about Canada, and they are unilaterally intemperate and ill-informed. That said, I'm with Doyle: I can't wait to get it. I think it is important to keep an eye on the unilaterally intemperate and ill-informed, especially when they happen to be running the latest competitor for cable news supremacy.

Fox was the first network to declare Bush president in 2000, and Roger Ailes and the gang have been singing his praises ever since, and lavishing invective on the old media, the liberal media, like CNN. The Fox News Channel markets itself as the news for people who don't trust the news. One Fox survey found that only 14 percent of the respondents trusted the media. The military, the president, the public school system, and the Catholic church—even in the throes of its pedophilia scandal—all inspired more trust than the media. The only institution that polled worse than the media was big corporations, which is kind of funny given that Fox is a big media corporation. But the poll was part of Fox's ongoing effort to position itself as news for people who don't like the news. The Fox News Channel has aggressively marketed itself as the unbiased alternative to all the other news, with the tagline "We report, you decide" and frequent brags about their "fair and balanced" coverage. Fox's top-rated show, *The O'Reilly Factor,* markets itself as a No-Spin Zone, but it features a host who bellows about socialists and traitors, who bullies his guests and tells them to shut up when they disagree with him. It is popular precisely because O'Reilly is a reactionary loudmouth, not because he's Mr. Neutral. CNN maintains the credibility edge in this battle of the broadcast titans, but they too have made their broadcasts louder, flashier, and quicker, so as not to be totally trounced by the belligerent Fox juggernaut.

It should be noted that the very idea that journalists should be neutral or objective is a fairly recent one. America's earliest papers were fiercely partisan. The invention of the telegraph and the founding of the Associated Press helped standardize coverage in the late nineteenth century. But for the great turn-of-the-century newspaper tycoons, like Joseph Pulitzer and William Randolph Hearst, a newspaper was a platform and a project as much as it was a moneymaking enterprise. During the heyday of yellow journalism, both editors trafficked in sensation and scandal as they fought for readers and meddled in political events, like the Spanish-American War. During

World War II, the FCC's "Mayflower laws" discouraged editorializing. Over the course of the forties, however, this no-editorializing policy seemed too restrictive, and changed into an equal time policy, otherwise known as the fairness doctrine, in 1949. Equal time refers to election laws that require networks to give opposing candidates for office equal airtime to get their messages out. The fairness doctrine was less binding, being a FCC guideline rather than a law, but it meant that media outlets had to make an effort to present both sides of a controversial issue, and give all interested parties the opportunity to speak out. Editorial content was supposed to be evenhanded, and reportage was supposed to be neutral. The idea that reporters would traffic only in facts and figures made it possible for the new news owners to distance themselves from editorial content, and present and sell the news as independent and professional. Television's ability to air footage also helped the turn toward just-the-facts journalism.

The fairness doctrine was the object of furious debate during the Reagan administration. Opponents of the doctrine, like right-wing think tanks, argued that airing both sides of every issue was a violation of the First Amendment, and actually discouraged coverage of controversial issues. Supporters of the doctrine pointed out that it actually stipulated that the broadcasters cover issues that were important to the public, and made broadcasters present a range of opinions about these issues. Reagan vetoed the fairness doctrine in 1987, and then Bush the Elder threatened to veto it again when Democrats brought it up in 1991. In 1993, when the Democrats tried to revive the fairness doctrine, right-wingers spun this effort as the Hush Rush bill. There's a little truth in that spin; Reagan's deregulation of the FCC spawned tons of right-wing radio shows. In January of 2005, during the course of a House debate on the FCC and indecency fines, Democratic members such as Louise Slaughter called, once again, for the reinstatement of the fairness doctrine. Given the majorities in the House and the Senate, this seems highly unlikely. The FCC is more interested in Janet Jackson's boob, and pandering to the latest wave of culture warriors, than it is in fostering broader public discourse, or more evenhanded coverage.

Few of us still think that the media are objective or neutral, but there are plenty of arguments about exactly which way that bias skews. Liberals say that the corporate press corps is inherently right-wing, and that journalists have become the toadying and fawning lackeys of power, reluctant to expose the excesses and trespasses of their owners and advertisers. Right-wingers decry the touchy-feely liberal media that likes gays, minorities, feminists, and big government, but shits all over guns, God, country, and money. Both are right and wrong. Professionals in the media do tend to vote Democratic, and to be fairly liberal on social issues. However, those who run media organizations tend to be right-wing, like Rupert Murdoch, or corporate interests, like GE, owners of NBC.

The idea that the media are a bunch of commies has long been a favorite thumping tub on talk radio, where the voices range from the right wing to the paleolithically right wing, including freshly chatty types like G. Gordon Liddy and Oliver North—I guess the airwaves have opened them up in ways that being under oath never could. According to a study conducted by the Joan Shorenstein Center on the Press, Politics and Public Policy, 40 percent of viewers think that the media has a liberal bias, and 32 percent think that the media's bias is conservative. Content analyses of CNN and Fox show that they're actually both pretty conservative. Fox is more right-wing on social issues, but both channels are equally likely to shake their pompoms for the Bush administration. The right wing certainly bellows louder, and is insistent that the default mode of the media is liberal. The usage of the word *liberal* as an epithet has long been part of the right's media strategy. They call this strategy playing the ref, and it is the preferred technique of professional right-wing bloviators like O'Reilly, Ann Coulter, and Rush Limbaugh. First, you argue that all the media suffers a liberal bias. Then, you argue that your views are not getting the fair hearing they deserve thanks to those rotten, biased liberals, even though you just so happen to be saying all this during your millionth TV appearance.

The overwhelming majority in the Shorenstein study thought that the media were biased, but they summed up media bias not in partisan terms, but with other words, bummer words like *negative, cynical,* and *depressing.* The really bad thing about the news is not that it favors a specific political agenda, but that the news is always bad. All the tales of crime and sleaze and misery don't just bum people out. These bleeding leads inevitably crowd out news about other crucial social issues. For example, the labor beat is long gone. When reporters write about work, they don't write about jobs or working conditions, they write about careers, management, or investments. The growth of prime-time newsmagazines has led to more coverage of celebrities, crime, lifestyles, and health, not in-depth coverage of education, the economy, military policy, and domestic and foreign affairs.

Certain politicians may enjoy extended press honeymoons, particularly during wartime, but political coverage in general is reflexively negative, a steady stream of dismal plotting and posturing. Media critic James Fallows notes that people and media people talk about politics in two entirely different ways. In election campaigns, when people are invited to ask questions in

202 **Your Call Is Important to Us**

town hall programs, they tend to ask about the what of politics.
They want to know what the candidates are going to do about
specific problems affecting their communities. Journalists always look for the how of politics, the strategic angle, the spin.
You don't hear about how any given policy or issue affects citizens, or voters, only how it affects the campaign. Covering politics as a horse race may seem more exciting than simply
explaining the political process to people, but it only serves to
distance people further from the political process, and reduces
democracy to a game played by the powerful few. The more the
press describes politicians as corrupt to a man, the less interest
readers have in politics. This is a very dangerous cycle, for the
press and politics both, since they are ultimately dependent on
one another. People who care about politics are far more likely
to follow the news, and people who follow the news are far
more likely to care about politics.

This is why the news is fundamentally unlike all the other
shows. Even though the news is sold like any other program,
with an eye to ratings, demographic wedges, and the concerns
of advertisers, it is not like other programs. A free press is an in-
tegral part of a democracy, and the media have a greater role to
play than simply raking in the bucks and the ratings. Thomas
Jefferson said that if you could only have one or the other,
democracy or a press, he'd take the free press. The media still
sees itself as a watchdog, and is forever telling us that it's on our
side, getting all worked up into a lather on our behalf. It's just a
shame that so much of that perfectly good anger and attention
has been squandered on trifles like sharks and kidnappers, on
stories that fondle the feelings and bypass the brain.

A study on press credibility, conducted by the American
Society of Newspaper Editors, found that more than three-
quarters of the people they polled believed that the media spent

too much time on scandalous stories because they were sexy or exciting, not because they were actually important stories. Scandals may provide a cheap, quick ratings boost, but they ultimately erode the credibility of the profession, and audience for the product, particularly when the scandals are presented as newsworthy simply for being scandals. When you do sleazy stories in a sloppy fashion, the slime can't help but stick. Journalists are no longer perceived as the cigar-chomping, fedora-sporting champions of the common man, and, before their post–September 11 boost, they ranked somewhere around lawyers, insurance salesmen, and politicians in polls about public trust.

When the media does assume the advocacy role, it's often against an itsy-bitsy bugbear, issues more appropriate to a small claims court. Or we are driven into a tizzy about some unlikely scourge, like the West Nile virus. Or we are presented with ridiculous duct-tape solutions to Orange Terror Alert problems. We get the shocked and appalled, but we rarely hear how we could make things less shocking or appalling. The news always happens to someone else, and the farther away they are, the less we care, unless they're already famous.

I'm not saying there's no news out there. In fact, the great paradox is that you can drown in news if you care to. This is a great time to be a news junkie, if you're willing to do a little digging. The public broadcasters, like PBS, NPR, CBC, and the BBC, have gotten a little flashier, but they still do excellent investigative work on programs like *Frontline* and *The Fifth Estate*, and air longer, more thoughtful pieces than your average cable blip. The Internet, in particular, is a news junkie's dream. Most of the world's major papers and broadcasters are but a click away, which is not even to mention the countless online-only news sources. One of the frustrating things about the fake

Web page look of the new cable news channels is that it assumes that people like the Web because they can get lots of short little bursts of info. This misses what people really love about the Web, which is the sheer abundance of information from a plurality of sources.

The blogosphere is beginning to overlap with the MSM in all sorts of curious ways. Perhaps the best example of the collision between the old media and the new media is Rathergate. In September 2004, *60 Minutes* did a show on Bush's Texas National Guard Service, or lack thereof. Right-wing bloggers began questioning the validity of the documents the report was based on, and their concerns migrated back to the MSM. CBS admitted that it probably shouldn't have aired the show without making sure the documents were kosher. Dan Rather apologized. Right-wing blogs rejoiced, and took Rathergate as a sign of their triumph over the lumbering, liberal MSM.

Blogs make no pretense to objectivity, but their flagrant partisanship is part of their charm, particularly when compared to Fox's disingenuous claims of neutrality. Even though banners and pop-up ads are irritating, the information-to-ad ratio on the Web is as good as, if not better than, that of newspapers. It remains to be seen how long the Internet will remain a haven for independent media providers and a cheap conveyance for heaps of information. The usual suspects are rubbing their hands and wondering how, exactly, they can fashion the Internet into something infinitely more profitable and obedient. The cable companies and the Baby Bells are successfully lobbying the FCC for more telecommunications deregulation. In June 2003, the FCC suggested further relaxation of media ownership rules, allowing companies to own more outlets in the same markets, and to own both broadcasters and newspapers, even if that makes the company in question that city's only news source. The motion passed by a margin of 3–2, and has since been contested by the commissioners who were outvoted, in the Senate and Supreme Court, and by millions of angry activists who think the media are consolidated enough, thanks. The 1996 Telecommunications Act, the last major bout of FCC deregulation, set the stage for almost-monopoly control of phone service, and the subsequent expansion and collapse of WorldCom, the second biggest phone behemoth. You probably heard about WorldCom in the news, but you probably didn't hear so much as a syllable about the 1996 Telecommunications Act—yawn—and how it made a crisis like WorldCom possible. A corporate corruption story is a good story. An explanation of the effects of industry deregulation, particularly when media giants want more of the same, is not a good story.

You can watch TV news, or read your lousy local chain paper, and not get very much news at all. They're like fruit drinks, colored sugar water with 10 percent juice. I don't know what your particular "action" or evening news shows are like, but all the ones I've seen are pretty much the same. There's maybe five or ten minutes of local news, and five or ten minutes of rehashed world news, if you can make it past the forty minutes of advertising, inane banter, chummy chuckling, grimaces of solemn concern, promos and teasers for upcoming stories, and health and lifestyle stories that are, more often than not, video news releases produced by PR companies hired by companies that produce health and lifestyle products. The audience for local news has decreased to 59 percent of those who watch the news, but local newscasts remain lean, mean profit machines, with solid ad revenues and increasingly frugal production values. People watch them out of sheer force of habit. They don't make you think, but they do make the bucks.

Despite all the fluff and sleaze and doom and gloom, people haven't given up on the news. In fact, the good news about the news is that 80 percent of Americans still pay attention to it daily, for about an hour on average. But the bad news about that good news is that most of those people watching the news are fossils— meaning anyone over the age of thirty-five. Old people love news, and they tend to get their news from old-school sources, like the newspaper. Young people are the least likely to pay any attention whatsoever to the news. Less than a quarter of people under thirty read the newspaper, and the numbers for those aged thirty to forty aren't much better, hovering around 30 percent. People aren't picking up the paper as they grow older and be- come more responsible. In fact, the thirtysomethings spent more time reading the papers when they were in their twenties, and have drifted away from print journalism over the past decade.

When youngsters do consult the news, they tend to graze, checking out the breaking stories on CNN or Fox, finding something on the Web, listening to the radio on the drive to work, or laughing at a topical gag on a late-night show. *The New York Times Magazine* ran a fretful cover story about how kids these days seem to be getting all their news from David Letterman and *The Daily Show*. In *The Daily Show*'s defense, the nice people who make *The Daily Show* are the first to tell you that they are a fake news show, and that you should watch the real news, too. Most *Daily Show* viewers do; one study found that they were actually better informed about current events than those watching the big three newscasts or cable news. *The Daily Show* may be hilarious, but it also covers a lot of hard news stories, and has a Peabody to show for it, which is more than you can say for Bill O'Reilly.

But I digress. The move to softer news, the increased use of graphics, titles, and soundtracks, and the shrinking of sound bites to blips on a crawl are all attempts to cater to the grazers, desperate attempts to reach out to that elusive, lucrative youth market. The drive for better ratings is not simply a matter of getting more people to watch your show. Would that it were so simple. The big question is, who are the people watching your show? Are they young, attractive types, or are they demographically undesirable fogeys? This is important for advertisers, since the youthful contingent is their holy grail, worth two or three times as much cash as their elders. It seems very ass-backwards, insofar as older people have way more access to money and credit than young people, but the theory is that if you get them young, you've got their money for life, so get them young you must.

Cable news picks up more of the kids than the big three, but the average age of a regular Fox News Channel or CNN viewer is still about forty-four, a decade moldier than the cut-off for the chosen market, eighteen to thirty-four. *CNN Headline News* was built for the express purpose of luring those recalcitrant, media-resistant kids. One exec said that the channel was perfect for the way the youth viewed news, since they could dip in and grab a dab of all the trouble in the world. Heaven forfend that programmers detain the little ADD-lings for twenty-two straight minutes of news, or forty-four agonizing minutes of documentary exposition. Why, these young people went from *Sesame Street* to MTV to video games and the Web, and they demand constant stimulation, staccato bursts of super-cool content, 24–7. To get their attention, you need dancing numbers, you need irony and technology, you need to make the news fun. So, *Headline News* has a faux-Internet busy screen, which features a foxy talking head, alternating with short texts and big graphics, framed by a succession of insipid headlinettes, a weather graphic, and a sports scoreboard graphic. It's too much information and too little information at the same time, an unholy stew of War on Terror and freaky deaths and truncated quotes from White House spokespeople and celebirthdays and box-office totals, shorn of any and all context. You never see a story longer than a sentence, and the writing staff favors bad puns and lame pop culture gags, like "Hussein on the Membrane," for a story about Saddam. They're aiming it right at relative whippersnappers like me, but I can't dip in for more than five minutes at a time lest I rouse the nervous tic in my right eyelid. In May of 2003, they ran repeated coverage of the man with the longest ear hair in the world. Freakish? Certainly. News? No. We were having a couple of wars and a corporate crime wave back then. Those things are, y'know, newsy.

Fifteen minutes here and fifteen minutes there, especially if it's fifteen minutes of adverinfotainment, is a flimsy basis for formulating an informed opinion on any matter of consequence. If you strafe people with short, flashy things, their capacity and willingness to pay heed to long, dullish things diminishes from lack of use. Reading the headline of a news story is like reading the title of a book. It's a good start, but that's about it. Dumbing it down for the kiddies, a tried, tested, and true marketing strategy from blockbuster films, is not a good idea for the news. Any time a serious news organization tries hard to be cool, they end up coming off like your grandma rapping, which is to say, deeply awkward and decidedly uncool. Making the news a fun cool thing like all the other fun cool things gives people the option to treat the news like other shows, watchable or unwatchable based on how much you enjoy watching it, a game the news will always lose. When news organizations dumb the stories down for the kiddies, they also make sure that they will never, ever grow up. A *PBS*

Online NewsHour forum on youth and the media featured one posting by a teenage girl who said that teens like her want to hear more about depressing stuff like war in Afghanistan and murder trials—*not*! Instead, she suggested, the news should show more upbeat stories, like a new polar bear being born at the zoo. A baby bear? Save that shit for the Discovery Channel. That is *not* news. And we shouldn't make it news to please idiots of all ages who are like, ew, the news is hard and war is so totally depressing. Another post offered a helpful suggestion for the disgruntled teen. She should really try *Headline News,* said a CNN exec. It was perfect for busy people like her.

CHAPTER TEN

THINK OF THE CHILDREN!

or Life During Wartime

Convictions are more dangerous enemies of the truth than lies.

—FRIEDRICH NIETZSCHE

This has been an easy book to write and an impossible book to end. New shit just keeps pushing the old shit into obsolescence. This is usually the part of the book where the author offers practical solutions: I've got nothing. I am not a problem solver. I am a crank. It was lovely to discover, however, that I am not merely a crank. This book is only the tip of the shit I sifted through, which is but the teensiest pore on the great Godzilla of bullshit.

Although I am Canadian, this book wound up being primarily about American bullshit, which is much more ubiquitous, well funded, and outrageous. Canada thinks America is loud and dumb, and America thinks Canada is lame and boring, but they are still brothers, raised with shared Enlightenment family values, like freedom of the press, free markets, and democracy. Canada venerates moderation, while the Yanks excel at extremes: the best and the worst, the richest and the poorest, the puritans and the pornographers, all living cheek by jowl.

America is also at a particularly bullshitty moment in its own history. Since I started cobbling this book together, in 2001, America has been in war mode, and war and bullshit go together like peanut butter and jelly, gin and tonic, or Oceania and Eastasia and Eurasia. The word *bullshit* first appeared in a dictionary as American vulgar slang in 1915, but some etymologists argue that the term was popularized during the world wars, overtaking previous epithets like chickenshit. Moreover, I think that the vast bullshit-disseminating apparatus is a descendant of the war propaganda deployed in the service of both world wars. Bernays, the father of PR, learned the rudiments of his trade working for the government, bolstering the war effort that happened at home, the war for the hearts and minds. Be they Axis or Allies, nations at war produce gross buckets of propaganda and moral suasion. They have to. You can't convince people to sign up for something so ruinous and costly without euphemisms and evasions— strong rhetoric about impending danger and/or a just cause.

The Bush administration is the latest in a long line of wartime bullshitters. When the threat-based justifications for the war, like weapons of mass destruction, were proven to be false or exaggerated, the administration simply switched emphasis, pushing the just cause and the spread of freedom and democracy. In Bush's 2005 inaugural speech—which was pretty short—he used the word *freedom* twenty-five times and *liberty* fifteen times. Freedom, and the glorious struggle for liberty, is a classic war speech theme. How do you disagree with it? Everybody except evildoers likes freedom. Even though the Bush administration has curtailed civil liberties in a host of ways, it consistently wraps itself in the flag of freedom and liberty. It also uses the rhetoric of freedom to push its domestic agenda; whether the issue is tax cuts or the privatization of Social Security, Bush spins it as freeing people to spend their own money and make their own choices.

What I find really pernicious about this is not just the fact that Bush bullshits, like every politician. Bush and company distinguish themselves by *believing* their own bullshit. I don't think Paul Wolfowitz was spinning when he said that American troops would be welcomed in the Middle East as liberators. I think he actually thought that, and refused to entertain evidence to the contrary. This is the other big problem with the Bush regime: It brooks no dissent, and does not take kindly to being called on its bullshit. Moderate Republicans like Paul O'Neill, Christine Todd Whitman, and Colin Powell have been driven out of the government for questioning, or disagreeing with, the policy initiatives of the inner circle. Several commentators have noted that this inner circle is as clenched and concealed as a sphincter.

In a chilling October 2004 *New York Times Magazine* article, writer Ron Suskind detailed Bush's distaste for debate, and reliance on instinct and religion to the detriment of evidence or fact. One of Bush's aides mocked Suskind's attachment to quaint notions like facts and evidence, and the writer's allegiance to "the reality-based community": "That's not the way the world really works anymore," he continued. "We're an empire now, and when we act, we create our own reality. And while you're studying that reality—judiciously, as you will—we'll act again, creating other new realities, which you can study too, and that's how things will sort out. We're history's actors . . . and you, all of you, will be left to just study what we do."

In your face, you fact-loving pussies! Have fun studying us, losers, while we remake the world in our image and then re-make it again. This attitude gives me the heebie-jeebies, and I am not alone. The phrase "reality-based community" has mi-grated to the blogosphere, where progressive bloggers declare themselves proud members.

The declaration that the empire is creating its own reality, and that the rest of us can just take notes, is not just bullshit but meta-bullshit, bullshit about bullshitting. The disdain for the reality-based community is merely the latest manifestation of a long and successful campaign of right-wing reality creation, of bullshitting about their own bullshit. For example, Bush and his ilk have done an excellent job of redefining certain words, like elitist, conservative, and liberal. Elite used to mean some-body with lots of wealth and power, like, say, Dick Cheney. Now elite means somebody who reads books and indulges in hated nuance, like that ol' flip-flopper John Kerry. Bush and the gang are not conservatives in the traditional, Burkean sense of hav-ing respect for established authority and tradition. They may be social conservatives, but more than anything else they are free-market radicals, who dismantle established programs rather than conserving them. Some are bloody anarchists. Talk to the kid at the protest rally with all the anarchy symbols on his jacket, and you will probably discover that he wants more gov-ernment, like fairer trade regulations. Grover Norquist wants to drown the government in a tub.

Even though the United States and Canada are founded on the liberal principles of the Enlightenment, like freedom and democracy, the word *liberal* has been hijacked and turned into a synonym for treasonous America-hater. Bush's insistence that America was founded on Christian faith is historically in-accurate; most of the Founding Fathers were Deists, who put far more faith in reason than they did in religion. Paine, for example, famously declared that the only church he needed was the one in his head. Jefferson edited his own Bible, which kept Jesus' practical moral teachings and tossed out all the dogma and supernatural events. Sure, they believed in a benevolent Creator, but they were also pretty serious about the separation of church and state, for the benefit of both institutions. After the election, historian Garry Wills wrote an editorial for the *New York Times* that the reelection of Bush marked a turn away from the Enlightenment, and a turn towards theocracy and blind faith. His claim might be a tad hyperbolic, but it is not without merit. Bush's declaration that freedom is a gift God gives us all skips a step in the old Deist formula. God gives us reason, and then we use that blessed faculty to build states that foster and protect freedom. The Bible certainly didn't lay the groundwork for free and democratic societies. Reason did. Liberals did. And I do not trust Bible-thumpers to maintain their precious legacy.

As Bush's aide noted, history's actors are not bound. They are not bound by history, obviously, nor are they bound by truth and facts. They are not bound by costs, either. Another bullshit aspect of this war is that the costs of war are being kept, like a CEO's stock options, off the books. The 2005 budget did not include costs for operations in Iraq. The $2.5 trillion budget slashed social services, including education, in an attempt to reduce the ever-swelling deficit, but experts are still projecting it will rise to over $400 billion this year, before military costs are factored in. Spending for the U.S.'s Iraqi adventure is over $150 billion, and Bush has recently requested another $80 billion toward the cost of rebuilding Iraq. Who is going to pay for all this? Not Bush, and not Cheney, but the generations to come, that's who.

One of the reasons why war needs bullshit is to cover up the gruesome, unnatural truth: Wars gorge themselves on the young. Most of the soldiers fighting this war are young and poor. Jessica Lynch couldn't even celebrate her homecoming with a beer, being two years shy of the legal drinking age. The deficits that Bush is racking up, for war costs and tax cuts and corporate welfare, are also burdens that the youth will have to bear. When MoveOn ran a contest called Bush in 30 Seconds to solicit ads opposing the president's reelection, the winning entry, Child's Pay, made this case graphically, showing kids toiling in factories and washing dishes to pay down billions in Bush debt.

I'm not surprised the ad with the little spuds won. "Think of the children" is the ultimate equal-opportunity piety, invoked in the name of lefty causes like gun control and the environment, and of right-wing ones like censorship and the drug war. Bush has been selling his plan to privatize Social Security as an intervention on behalf of children's retirement funds. On the morning of September 11, when he first heard news of the attacks, Bush was, as everyone knows, in an elementary-school classroom reading to little kids. Education has long been one of his pet causes—leave no child behind!—but his policies hurt kids now, and will have deleterious effects on them in the future.

Bush engages in think-of-the-childrenism because every politician does. Children are the last innocents in our hopelessly profaned world. Though I have met little tiny assholes, I do not recommend expressing such sentiments aloud. It is a commonplace that crimes against kids are the worst crimes of all. Chester the Molester is the guy most likely to be beaten to a pulp by crackheads and murderers in jail. And when he gets out of jail, he is the criminal most likely to inspire furious poster campaigns by the residents of his new neighborhood.

Throughout the past few years, even as the war machine trundled on, the news ran beaucoup de endangered child stories, about kiddies snatched from bedrooms by strangers or fondled by Catholic priests. When prudes freaked out about Janet Jackson's boob, they did so in the name of the children.

You can see our tender care for the youth in the way that we market heart attacks on buns directly at the little darlings, so that every time they pass a golden arch, the begging begins. You can feel the love for the young in each new product line, each new buddy like Barney and Elmo and SpongeBob, available in TV, book, movie, CD, T-shirt, plush, plastic, and cereal form. You can see plain evidence of our concern in the millions of children who live in grievous poverty. You can also see the love in the gentle attentions of the juvenile justice system and the lavish hands of our speed-dispensing kiddie shrinks. You can really see the love in the way that we work increasingly long hours and spend less and less time with our beloved kids, leaving them plunked in front of a blinky box munching neon crud for hours at a time. And then there's the way we glut ourselves on nonrenewable resources like oil and clean water and arable land and blithely keep churning out smog and sludge and trash for an unspecified somebody to clean up . . . later. Think of the children? Don't make me laugh myself new holes. We're lucky if we can think of next Monday.

One of the reasons why think-of-the-childrenism enervates me is that I spend long hours with people's children. Don't worry, by the time I get my hands on them, they are in college, almost adults, and already ruined. Many are working way too many hours outside the classroom just to pay for class, or putting themselves into major hock before they've had their first legal bender. Plenty have no desire whatsoever to be there, and are merely in school because that is what you gotta do to get a good job. Several emerge from high school without a clue about stringing together a paragraph or reading and interpreting a complex document, and many of them view reading as a chore, rather than a necessary survival skill, or one of the world's great pleasures. I'm not saying your kids are dumb or lazy. Most of the kids I have taught, from the D students to the A pluses, have been perfectly delightful. They have just been marinating in ease, soaking in fun and cool, and so what's boring and hard is all the boringer and harder.

I am not the only concerned university educator out there, fretting about the decline of literacy and standards. The American Council of Trustees and Alumni is a group of virtuecrats that advocate for academic freedom, more history in the schools, and university accountability. The group, co-founded by Second Lady Lynne Cheney, issued a report in 2001 called "Defending Civilization: How Our Universities Are Failing America and What Can Be Done About It." It is a real humdinger. The report collects more than a hundred comments from seditious university professors in the wake of 9–11, which are mostly innocuous, wishy-washy root-cause stuff, like the suggestion that we ought to use our strength for peace, not war. The report thoroughly excoriates the academics for holding such views; rather than serve the cause of liberty, Ivory Tower nerds choose to BLAME AMERICA FIRST. Their caps, not mine.

Let us leave aside the absurdity of an organization ostensibly devoted to academic freedom censuring the insufficient jingoism of the Ivory Tower set. Let's consider the corrective. What, they ask, is to be done about Professor Granola, and Doctor Peacenik? Well, the angelic doctors who make up the ACTA think that kids should be learning about Lady Liberty's glorious past, boning up on their Western Civ instead of absorbing all that trendy hogwash about postcolonialism and postmodernity. Consequently, the report enthusiastically endorses great-books programs. It just so happens that I am also an enthusiastic endorser of great-books programs, being both a product and a teacher of one, but reading all those canonical books by Dead White Males sure didn't make me a patriot or a Republican. I may be a positively arteriosclerotic conservative when it comes to syllabi, but it is, in part, my time as a Western Civ nerd that makes me revile the shoddy fraudulence of everything else that the cons stand for and continue to perpetrate.

You don't really want the kids to take up and read, Lynne, believe me. That would totally fuck with the obfuscation and ignorance upon which your husband's fortune and the rest of his regime depend. Just think of all the subversive material in a great-books program. Young kids might pick up Plato's *Republic* and read about how democracy, though the most attractive and colorful form of political life, is fundamentally unstable and gives way to tyranny. The kids might notice how hard a task it was to found the Roman Empire, *secundum* Vergil. They might notice that usurers, rather than waiting for nations to come bow and scrape for their credit ratings, wander the burning sands in Dante's *Inferno*, and that barrators, those who profit from political office, are sunk in a *bolgia* of boiling pitch, eternally poked and tortured by demons. They might notice that the last round of major Allah vs. Jesus-my-God-is-bigger-than-your-God smackdowns raged on for at least five centuries. They might encounter inconveniently stringent statements like Kant's "to be truthful in all declarations is, therefore, a sacred and unconditionally commanding law of reason that admits of no expediency whatsoever." This is not even to mention the latter half of your average great-books year, which includes skeptics like Hume, liberals like

Mill, commies like Marx, scientists like Darwin, and atheists like Nietzsche. Even a cursory reading of such texts by middling students may well leave the beloved children scratching their heads after the latest State of the Union address.

ACTA is only one of the groups taking academia to task. Right-wing activist David Horowitz has recently been campaigning for an Academic Bill of Rights, to protect the youth from the fulminations of Professor Peacenik. Horowitz does a swell job of spinning this crusade into a fight for academic freedom and intellectual diversity, but it is actually a right-wing assault on one of the last bastions of genuine liberalism in American culture. Having successfully captured all three branches of government, the judiciary, and a goodly chunk of the media and public discourse, the right now wishes to seize academia, too, to protect their children from the trauma of having a hippie professor. Professor Stanley Fish, who has written several essays arguing that the university should be an apolitical environment, devoted solely to the search for knowledge, has described Horowitz's Bill of Academic Rights as a Trojan horse. Under the guise of diversity, the bill calls for more right-wing professors, and tells liberal professors to stuff a sock in it.

The right's latest poster boy for the radical corruption of academe is a real doozy, a Colorado professor of ethnic studies named Ward Churchill, who does not have a PhD, and who might be a fake American Indian. Churchill wrote an essay after 9–11 that referred to the victims of the WTC attack as "little Eichmanns." Bad taste? Certainly. But the pro-life movement has been taking the Holocaust's name in vain for years; tenured radicals do not have the monopoly on bogus Nazi comparisons. When O'Reilly and the gang got their hands on the offending essay in 2005, years after it was published, Churchill became the symbol of everything wrong with tenure and the professoriate in general. The right let out a mighty hue and cry. We pay those traitors' salaries! And they have our children!

As someone who has spent her whole life in academia, let me say that the right wing's claims are, as usual, exaggerated. Humanities faculties may skew left of the current American political dial, but the Ward Churchills are few and far between. And if you take a walk over to the business or law schools, you will find plenty of conservative hatchlings. Universities don't have the time and resources to be Marxist indoctrination camps. Most professors are far, far too busy trying to teach skills like essay writing, which students did not learn in their underfunded high schools, to foment the rise of the revolutionary proletariat. But this vilification of universities by the right is already starting to affect their own children's education. A colleague who had the pleasure of teaching in the American South told me his students said that their ministers and parents had warned them about university professors and their wicked ways. They were supposed to keep their heads down, get good grades, and not listen to the liberal claptrap. If you check out a right-wing message board like Free Republic, you will see the same advice. Until the university changes and expresses the right's worldview, the kids of cons are encouraged to detach themselves from the educational experience. This advice is about as anti-intellectual as it gets.

This right-wing incursion into university politics is disturbing because education is our only hope. I know I said I wasn't going to offer any solutions. But if there is one thing that can stem the tide of bullshit or reduce its deleterious effects, it is a critical and well-educated populace that knows its own language well enough to know when that language is being abused and misused. Education also helps facilitate income mobility, combating the erosion of the middle class. Even Bush says so. When, in the debates, the president was asked about income inequality, he immediately began talking about education programs like No Child Left Behind as a corrective. This was a classic Bush swerve away from a question he cannot answer, but there was a grain of truth in it. Education does help people move on up, provided they can afford the cover charge at the door, which is getting steeper and more onerous. Bush's rhetoric on education is nice, but his policies have been underfunded and wrongheaded, pushing teachers to teach to standardized tests. This kind of test-based curriculum is precisely why I have to teach eighteen-year-olds how to write complete sentences.When people cannot own and operate their own language, they are that much more susceptible to bullshit.

The bullshit pandemic is not a mystery. We are under the rule of pusillanimous, self-serving prevaricators, and thus, pusillanimous, self-serving prevarication is the rule. There's more shame and misery in being broke than in being fake. Why not bullshit? If it's good enough for the captains of industry, the titans of politics, the Catholic church, the medical establishment, and the media, then it's good enough for you.

Let's look at the tally.

It's bullshit that private interests have eclipsed public goods.

It's bullshit that companies devote more time and money to telling us how great they are, or how desperately we need them, than to simply providing quality products and services.

It's bullshit that the fruits of the boom went largely to the richest of the rich, and that the poor were once again left sucking the mop.

It's bullshit that the law treats corporations as people, and allows artificial people to get away with things that real people would never even dream of doing. Increased wealth concentration and growing corporate power are the result of deregulation and generous tax policies, which can be attributed to the best government the big-money lobbies can buy. And the fact that government is bought and paid for by the fortunate few means that the rest of us do not trust politicians or engage in the political process.

It's bullshit that pharmaceutical companies and the insurance industry have succeeded in privatizing public issues, like access to health care, and turning them into very valuable cash cows. Major retailers and other service industry titans go on and on like it's all about you, the almighty customer, but they are far more interested in their bottom line than the time you spend holding the line, listening to the titular blah-dee-blah.

It's bullshit that discount shopping and phone service are how we will spend our time and money, and that serving and waiting are our glorious employment future.

It's bullshit that so much of the news is so resolutely newsless, particularly in a time when we are suffering no shortage of newsworthy—dare I even haul out a dusty Hegelianism like world-historical?—events.

Even as I shake my tiny fist, I dig my comfy couch, my big TV, my salty snacks, and all the other accoutrements of my plush and cushy First World life. It's just that my eyebrows are plum tuckered out from all the arching, and my peepers are strained from persistent rolling. I am weary of responding to the news in the negative double affirmative: "Yeah, right." No ad campaign, no wonder pill, no blockbuster movie, no celebrity, no candidate, no entertainment complex, no glorious blandishment can compensate for a lack of trust and the sense that all is a scam or a sham, for the feeling that one is being fooled and fobbed off. Neat stuff and air-conditioned comfort are pleasing, but must they come at the cost of this fog of fibs? Does our prosperity really depend on an edifice of phoniness, erected by the fortunate few in their best interests? I don't think so. Nevertheless, ads fudge and fake, companies overstate and omit, governments euphemize and evade, the media distort and dumb down, and we are exhorted to smile and shrug and return to our regularly scheduled shiny things.

One of the dangers of writing a book such as this, besides its unendability, is that one is invariably warbling to the choir, or at least for fellow musicians. If you picked up this book, you were probably a little pissed off already. You, Gentle Reader, are probably not one of the powerful malefactors of great bullshit, so all of this huffing and puffing is kind of like chastising kids for poor attendance at school. The kids who are congenitally un-there aren't around to hear you chew them out.

But in the event you are a perpetrator (and you know in your heart of hearts if you are), I say unto you: Shame. Shame! Have you no sense of decency? You take names in vain, and send legions of vain names into the world. And when you fuck with English, you are money-changing in my temple.

Notes

This book is the fruit of many hours of Googling, and of consulting a host of government and policy-wonk databases, reading newspapers, and looking at recent nonfiction books. I am deeply indebted to many fine researchers and publications. Web links are operative as of March 2005. The italicized phrase at the beginning of each citation refers to a key fact or idea in the chapter specified, and may not be an exact quotation from the text.

CHAPTER ONE

2 message discipline: Mark McKinnon, quoted in Jake Tapper, "Ari: Gone but Not Forgotten," Salon. com, May 19, 2003; online at www.salon. com/news/feature/2003/05/19/ari/.

2 *Burson-Marsteller:* Their Web address is www.bm.com.

5 *Harry Frankfurt:* See Harry Frankfurt, *On Bullshit* (Princeton University Press, 2005).

9 *Bullfighter:* Deloitte & Touche are no longer associated with Bullfighter, which can now be downloaded at www.fightthebull.com. See Jonathan Glater, "Holy Change Agent! Consultants Edit Out Jargon," *The New York Times,* June 14, 2003.

CHAPTER TWO

21 *Total U.S. ad spending:* Figures come from Robert J. Coen's *Insider's Report,* produced by the Universal McCann agency. The most recent report is available online at www.universalmccann .com/Insiders1204.pdf.

21   *global PR revenues:* PR revenue figures come from the Council of Public Relations Firms, online at www.prfirms.org/resources/rankings/2002_rankings.asp.

24   *Bill Hicks:* His scathing monologue against advertisers and marketers is from his 1992 show, *Revelations,* available on a DVD released by Rykodisc in 2004, *Bill Hicks Live.*

25   *Trojan horse of sweet melody:* See Nat Ives, "Marketing Meets Anti-Establishment Music," *The New York Times,* November 6, 2002.

26   *TiVo pop-ups:* See Jefferson Graham and Michelle Kessler, "Ads to Pop Up When TiVo Users Scan Past Commercials," *USA Today,* November 18, 2004.

27   *letter to John Lahr:* The lengthy anti-censorship letter appears in *Love All the People: Lyrics, Letters, Routines* (Soft Skull Press, 2004.)

28   *shift from ads to PR:* See Al and Laura Ries, *The Fall of Advertising and Rise of PR* (HarperBusiness, 2002).

28   *Credibility Index:* The index is online at www.prsa.org/_About/prsafoundation/nciIndex.asp?ident=prsa0.

29   *Code of Ethics:* The Code of Ethics is available at www.prsa.org/_About/ethics/pledge.asp?ident=eth6. A preamble notes that emphasis on enforcement of this code has been eliminated, and describes the pledge as a useful guide.

29   *Burson-Marsteller clients:* From Conal Walsh, "Fur Flies as Greenpeace Grandee Takes PR Shilling," *The Guardian,* January 13, 2002, business section.

30   *History of U.S. advertising:* See Jackson Lears, *Fables of Abundance: A Cultural History of Advertising* (Basic Books, 1995).

30   *History of PR:* See Stuart Ewen, *PR! A Social History of Spin* (Basic Books, 1998).

31–33 *Edward Bernays:* My account is based on Larry Tye's excellent biography, *The Father of Spin: Edward L. Bernays and the Birth of Public Relations* (Crown, 1998).

33   *Propaganda:* Bernays's book has been reissued with an introduction by Mark Crispin Miller (Ig Publishing, 2004).

34   *The Silver Anvil Award:* Case studies for winners from 2000 to present are available at www.prsa.org/_Awards/silver/index.asp?ident=sil0.

39 *Front groups and astroturfing:* See www.prwatch.org, and John
Stauber and Sheldon Rampton, *Toxic Sludge Is Good for You: Lies,
Damn Lies, and the Public Relations Industry* (Common Courage
Press, 1995).

40 *Medialink:* Their website has been revamped and now touts
"the spirit to turn promises into reality" at www.medialink
.com/mdlkRela.htm.

40 *pro-Bush letter to the editor:* See "Stupid Papers and GOP
Astroturf," at *Daily Kos,* Tuesday, August 17, 2004; online at
dailykos.com/story/2004/8/17/17029/2550.

40 *Office of National Drug Control Policy:* The Government
Accountability Office chastised the ONDCP for the VNRs and
using the term Drug Czar. The GAO report is online at
www.gao.gov/decisions/appro/303495.htm.

40 *Armstrong Williams:* See Howard Kurtz, "Administration Paid
Commentator: Education Department Used Williams to
Promote 'No Child' Law," *Washington Post,* January 9, 2005.

CHAPTER THREE

43 *longest bear market:* See John Waggoner and Adam Shell, "Bear
Turns a Baffling 3," *USA Today,* March 19, 2003.

43 *National Bureau of Economic Research:* The Recession Dating
Procedure is available online at www.nber.org/cycles/
recessions.html.

43 *economy remained sluggish:* See Steven Greenhouse, "Looks
Like a Recovery, Feels Like a Recession," *The New York Times,*
September 1, 2003.

43 *36 million Americans living in poverty:* See *Income, Poverty and
Health Insurance 2003,* from the U.S. Census Bureau. Available at
www.census.gov/hhes/www/income03.html.

43 *debt, as of January 2005:* See the Bureau of Public Debt's debt-to-
the-penny website for constant updates: www.publicdebt.treas
.gov/opd/opdpenny.htm.

43 *record-breaking trade deficit:* See the Census Bureau's February
10, 2005 report at www.census.gov/indicator/www/ustrade.html.

44 *get some ribs, Stretch:* See *Remarks by the President to the Press
Pool, Nothin' Fancy Café, Roswell, NM,* January 22, 2004; available

online at www.whitehouse. gov/news/releases/2004/01/
200401225.html.

45   *Wealth figures:* From Inequality.org, at www.inequality.org/
facts.html.

49   *Survey of Consumer Finances:* See more on the 1998 survey in a
January 2000 government bulletin, *Recent Changes in U.S. Family
Finances: Results from the 1998 Survey of Consumer Finances,* at
www.federalreserve.gov/pubs/bulletin/2000/0100lead.pdf.

51   *Ethical Funds:* There is a press release related to the lawsuit on
their website at www.ethicalfunds.com/do_the_right_
thing/about_ef/newsroom/2000_ articles/02_02_00.asp.

51   *The Facts on Saving and Investing:* Released by the SEC in 1999. It
is still on their website, at www.sec.gov/pdf/report99.pdf.

52   *28 percent of Americans owed more:* See Pew Research Center for
the People and the Press, "Economic Inequality Seen As Rising,
Boom Bypasses Poor," survey released June 21, 2001; online at
people-press.org/reports/display.php3?ReportID=8.

52   *Record number of bankruptcies:* See press release from the
Administrative Office of the U.S. Courts, August 18, 2003; at
www.uscourts.gov/Press_Releases/603b.pdf.

52   *margin debt:* See the Financial Markets Center chart on margin
debt, available online at www.fmcenter.org/site/apps/s/
content.asp?c=8fLGJTOyHpE&b=222624&ct=278485.

54   *CEO pay and stock performance:* See Scott Klinger, "The Bigger
They Come, The Harder They Fall: High CEO Pay and the Effect
on Stock Prices," United for a Fair Economy, April 6, 2001;
available online at www.faireconomy.org/press/2001/Bigger_
They_Come.pdf.

55   *Coca-Cola:* See *The Economist,* "Douglas Daft: The New Broom at
Coca-Cola," February 10, 2000, and "Who's Wearing the
Trousers?" September 6, 2001.

56   *CEO pay and downsizing:* See Scott Klinger, "The Bigger They
Come," cited above.

59   *increased by 201 percent:* See The Center for Budget and Policy
Priorities, "Two Decades of Extraordinary Gains for Affluent
Americans Yield Widest Income Gaps Since 1929, New Data
Indicates," Tuesday, September 23, 2003; at www.cbpp.org/
9-23-03tax-pr.htm.

60 *21 million underemployed:* See John E. Schwarz, "The Hidden Side of the Clinton Economy," *The Atlantic Monthly,* October 1998.

60 *long boom income increases:* See www.inequality.org/facts.html.

61 *pragmatics of tax policy favor the wealthy:* See David Cay Johnston, "IRS More Likely to Audit the Poor and Not the Rich," *The New York Times,* April 16, 2000.

61 *"real rich people":* See President Bush's remarks in Annandale, VA, on August 9, 2004; online at www.whitehouse.gov/news/releases/2004/08/20040809-3.html.

62 *13 percent debt service ratio:* See Alan Greenspan's February 23, 2004 speech, "Understanding Household Debt Obligations," available at www.federalreserve.gov/boarddocs/speeches/2004/20040223/default.html.

65 *decline of meritocracy:* See "Ever Higher Society Ever Harder to Ascend: Meritocracy in America," *The Economist,* December 29, 2004.

65 *mendacious math:* See Paul Krugman, *The Great Unraveling: Losing Our Way in the New Century* (W. W. Norton, 2003).

CHAPTER FOUR

68 *genius of capitalism:* O'Neill quoted in Eric Alterman and Mark Green, *The Book on Bush: How George W. Misleads America* (Viking, 2004).

69 *50 percent in consulting:* See Arthur Levitt's testimony before the Senate Subcommittee on Securities and Banking, September 28, 2000; online at www.sec.gov/news/testimony/ts152000.htm#P49_9309.

71 *corporate responsibility:* The White House website has not been updated since 2003, but it is still available at www.whitehouse.gov/infocus/corporateresponsibility/.

71 *Larry Thompson:* See Anitha Reddy, "Deputy AG Profited Before Stock Fell; Thompson Exercised Providian Options During Transition," *Washington Post,* August 2, 2002.

72 *corporate fraud task force:* See *Fact Sheet Second Year Anniversary of President Bush's Corporate Fraud Task Force,* Federal Document Clearing House, Federal Department and Agency Documents, Regulatory Intelligence Data, July 20, 2004.

74   *"very dangerous and very counterproductive"*: Gramm's remarks are part of the Conference Report in the Senate on Sarbanes-Oxley on July 25, 2002.

74   *super-sweet for accounting firms:* See Mark Jaffe and Peter Robison, "Sarbanes-Oxley Becomes 'Open Checkbook' for KPMG, Ernst &Young," at Bloomberg.com, November 4, 2004; online at www.Bloomberg.com/apps/news?pid=10000103&sid=aAlUCtlfw9DI&refer=us.

75–78 *corporate personhood:* See Thom Hartmann, *Unequal Protection: The Rise of Corporate Dominance and the Theft of Human Rights* (Rodale Books, 2004), and Joel Bakan, *The Corporation: The Pathological Pursuit of Profit and Power* (Free Press, 2004).

83   *The Economist:* See "Is Government Disappearing?" *The Economist,* September 27, 2001.

85   *corporate tax revenues:* See Joel Friedman, "The Decline of Corporate Tax Revenues," Center for Budget and Policy Priorities, October 24, 2003; online at www.cbpp.org/10–16–03tax.htm.

85   *$143 billion:* See Jonathan Weisman, "Senate Passes Corporate Tax Bill: Bush Plans to Sign $143 Billion in Cuts," *Washington Post,* October 12, 2004.

85–86 *Paul O'Neill:* See Ron Suskind, *The Price of Loyalty: George W. Bush, The White House, and the Education of Paul O'Neill* (Simon and Schuster, 2004).

86   *Enron paperweights:* See Rick Bragg, "Enron's Collapse: Workers Feel Pain of Layoffs and Added Sting of Betrayal," *The New York Times,* January 20, 2002.

CHAPTER FIVE

93   *Contract with America:* Text is still available online at www.house.gov/house/Contract/CONTRACT.html.

96   *latter-day radical Tom:* See Michael Weisskopf and David Maraniss, "Forging an Alliance for Deregulation," *Washington Post,* March 12, 1995.

96   *Tom DeLay:* See Lou Dubose and Jan Reid, *The Hammer: Tom DeLay, God, Money, and the Rise of the Republican Congress* (Public Affairs, 2004).

97   *"Gestapo of government":* See "What's Next for the EPA?" on *PBS NewsHour Online,* December 21, 1995; at www.pbs.org/ newshour/bb/environment/epa_12–21.html.

97   *gerrymandering:* See Jeffrey Toobin, "The Great Election Grab," *The New Yorker,* December 8, 2003.

98   *associates indicted:* See Sylvia Moreno, "Three DeLay Workers Indicted in Texas," *Washington Post,* September 22, 2004. See also Lou Dubose, "Justice Delayed," *Mother Jones,* November/ December 2004.

98   *ethics complaints:* See Charles Babington, "Ethics Panel Rebukes DeLay," *Washington Post,* October 1, 2004.

98   *changing their ethics rules:* See Charles Babington, "GOP Pushes Rule Change to Protect DeLay's Post," *Washington Post,* November 17, 2004. See also Carl Hulse, "House GOP Acts to Protect Chief," *The New York Times,* November 18, 2004.

98   *GOP reversed their decision:* See Carl Hulse, "After Retreat, GOP Changes House Ethics Rule," *The New York Times,* January 5, 2005.

99   *outgoing House ethics chair:* See Mike Allen, "House Ethics Chair Likely to Be Replaced," *Washington Post,* January 6, 2005.

99   *Project Relief:* See Jan Reid, "Sin of Emissions," *Mother Jones,* September/October 1996, and Michael Weisskopf and David Maraniss, "Forging an Alliance for Deregulation," cited above.

100   *K Street Project:* See Nicholas Confessore, "Welcome to the Machine," *Washington Monthly,* July/August 2003. See also Jim VanderHei and Juliet Eilperin, "Targeting Lobbyists Pays Off for GOP," *Washington Post,* June 26, 2003.

103   *about twenty-four thousand lobbyists:* See Alex Knott, "Lobbyists Bankrolling Politicians," Center for Public Integrity, May 6, 2004; online at www.public-i.org/bop2004/report.aspx?aid=273.

105   *campaign financing:* See www.opensecrets.org, the definitive campaign finance site, sponsored by the Center for Responsive Politics. See also Charles Lewis and the Center for Public Integrity, *The Buying of the President 2004* (Perennial, 2004).

106   *527s:* See "Silent Partners," Center for Public Integrity, online at www.public-i.org/527/.

CHAPTER SIX

115 *200 billion in 2002:* See IMS Health, "World Pharma Sales Growth: Slower but Still Steady," at www.imsglobal.com/insight/news_story/0302/news_story_030228.htm.

115 *17 billion:* See pharmiweb.com, "Going OTC in the USA," October 18, 2004; online at www.pharmiweb.com/Features/feature.asp?ROW_ID=508.

119 *Prairie Plant Systems:* For more details about Canada's medical marijuana contract, see the Office of Cannabis Medical Access at the Health Canada website, online at www.hc-sc.gc.ca/hecs-sesc/ocma/bckdr_3–0601.htm.

119 *Partnership for a Drug-Free America:* See Cynthia Cotts, "The Partnership: Hard Sell in the Drug Wars" *The Nation,* March 9, 1992.

120 *$2.7 billion:* The General Accounting Office issued a report on FDA supervision of DTC advertising in October 2002: "Prescription Drugs: FDA Oversight of Direct-to-Consumer Advertising Has Limitations," online at www.gao.gov/docdblite/details.php?rptno=GAO-03–177.

121 *80 percent of seniors:* See the special section on drugs in *Health: United States 2004,* National Center for Health Statistics, online at www.cdc.gov/nchs/hus.htm.

122 *Big Pharma, the most profitable sector:* See Marcia Angell, *The Truth About Drug Companies: How They Deceive Us and What to Do About It* (Random House, 2004).

123 *$500 billion, $800 billion:* See phrma.org, the website of the industry's advocacy group, the Pharmaceutical Researchers and Manufacturers of America. Summaries of the industry position on DTC ads, research costs, profits, and so forth are available online at www.phrma.org/publications/quickfacts/.

123 *Public Citizen report:* See "Rx R&D Myths: The Case Against the Drug Industry's R&D 'Scare Card,'" *Congress Watch,* July 2001; online at www.citizen.org/congress/campaign/special_interest/articles.cfm?ID=6538.

125 *New York Times:* See Kurt Eichenwald and Gina Kolata, "Drug Trials Hide Conflicts for Doctors," *The New York Times,* May 16, 1999.

126   *up to 370:* See the Public Citizen website. They have also launched a new site, worstpills.org, to keep track of potentially dangerous drugs like Vioxx and Celebrex.

129   *Prilosec and Nexium:* For more on the switch from Prilosec to Nexium, see Malcolm Gladwell, "High Prices: How to Think About Prescription Drugs," *The New Yorker,* October 10, 2004.

130   *SSRIs for kids:* See the FDA page "Antidepressant Use in Children, Adolescents and Adults," at www.fda.gov/cder/drug/antidepressants/default.htm.

132   *global patent debates:* See "Dying for Drugs" series in *The Guardian.* A good place to start is Sarah Boseley with James Atill, "Battle Over Cheap Drugs goes to WTO," July 16, 2001.

133   *Sarafem:* See Carla Spartos, "Sarafem Nation," *Village Voice,* December 6, 2000, and Lisa Belkin, "Prime Time Pushers," *Mother Jones,* March/April 2001.

137   *top ten killers:* See *Health: United States 2004,* National Center for Health Statistics, cited above.

138   *top ten sellers:* See IMS Health, at www.imshealth.com.

CHAPTER SEVEN

140   *Spitzer insurance probe:* See "Sins of Commission," *The Economist,* February 1, 2005.

146   *Premiums have gone up:* For comprehensive health insurance cost data, see the Kaiser Foundation website, www.kff.org.

146   *September 11:* See Robert P. Hartwig, "September 11: One Hundred Minutes of Terror That Changed the Global Insurance Industry Forever," Insurance Information Institute, online at www.iii.org/media/hottopics/insurance/ sept11/sept11paper/.

149   *Doctors have filed suit:* The Cigna and Aetna court case documents are available courtesy of the law offices of Archie Lamb, the class action lawyer involved with the case. Online at www.hmocrisis.com/courtdocuments.html.

149   *state-farm-sucks.com:* See Perry Z. Binder, "Domain Names and Your Company's Giant Sucking Sound," online at www.gsu.edu/~rmipzb/Domainarticle.pdf.

151   *45 million Americans:* See the page of links on health care and the uninsured at the Kaiser Family Foundation website, at www.kff.org/uninsured/index.cfm.

151   *The New England Journal of Medicine:* See Drs. Steffie Woolhandler and David Himmelstein, and Terry Campbell, "Costs of Healthcare Administration in the U.S. and Canada," August 21, 2003.

155   *Aetna settlement:* For documents related to Aetna's court cases and settlements, see Aetna's legal issues Web page, at www.aetna.com/legal_issues/index.html.

156   *CIGNA settlement:* See Tanya Albert, "Judge OKs CIGNA Settlement with Doctors," *Amednews.com,* February 24, 2003; at www.ama-assn.org/amednews/2004/02/23/prsd0223.htm.

156   *Aetna v. Davila:* Documents related to this case are also available on the Aetna website.

157   *patients' rights legislation:* See Dana Milbank and Juliet Eilperin, "On Patients' Rights Deal, Bush Scored with a Full-Court Press," *Washington Post,* August 3, 2001.

157   *Gramm-Leach-Bliley:* See the Financial Markets Center's in-depth coverage of the GLB, online at www.fmcenter.org/site/pp.asp?c=8fLGJTOyHpE&b=224816.

158   *Executive Life:* For more on the Executive Life scandal, see Ellie Winninghoff, "The French Connection," *Forbes,* September 2001, and "No Assurances," also by Winninghoff, in *Mother Jones,* January 2002.

159   *Leon Black:* See Bernard Condon, "Black is Back," *Forbes,* November 2004.

159   *600 million:* See "Accord Near in Suit Over Insurer's Sale," *Washington Post,* February 16, 2005.

160   *"passing the trash":* See Robert Lenzner, "Passing the Trash," *Forbes,* January 2000.

161   *Spitzer reinsurance probe:* See Thor Valdmanis, "AIG gets subpoenas from SEC, Spitzer," *USA Today,* February 14, 2005.

CHAPTER EIGHT

164   *Brookings Institution:* See William Fulton et al., "Who Sprawls Most? How Growth Patterns Differ Across the U.S.," Center for Urban and Metropolitan Policy, July 2001; online at

www.brookings.edu/dybdocroot/es/urban/publications/
Fulton.pdf.

166   *six billion square feet:* Figures from the International Council of
Shopping Centers, an industry group, online at www.icsc.org/
srch/rsrch/scope/current/index.php.

169   *$44 billion:* See the Annual Retail Trade Data at the U.S. Census
Bureau, available online at www.census.gov/svsd/www/
artstbl.html.

171   *Liza Featherstone:* See "Down and Out in Discount America" and
"Wal-Mart Values: Selling Women Short," *The Nation,* December
16, 2004, and December 16, 2002. Featherstone has also written a
book on the Dukes class action suit against Wal-Mart called
*Selling Women Short: The Landmark Battle for Workers' Rights at
Wal-Mart* (Basic Books, 2004).

171   *anti-Wal-Mart studies:* Al Norman's website, www.sprawl-busters.
com, is a comprehensive resource for research criticizing Wally
World.

172   *$15 billion:* For more on Wal-Mart and the trade deficit, check
out *Is Wal-Mart Good for America?* a November 2004 episode of
PBS's excellent *Frontline.* You can watch the show online at
www.pbs.org/wgbh/pages/frontline/shows/walmart/.

176   *more than $400,000:* See Simon Head, "Inside the Leviathan," *The
New York Review of Books,* December 16, 2004.

176   *Occupational Outlook Handbook:* Online at the Bureau of Labor
Statistics, www.bls.gov/home.htm.

178   *fifty thousand call centers:* See "The Vanishing American Call
Center," commweb.com, September 21, 2004; at www.commweb
.com/customercontact/47900751.

178   *Call Center Magazine:* See Brendan Read, "Finding a Home for Your
Call Center," *Call Center Magazine,* September 1999; online at
www.callcentermagazine.com/showArticle.jhtml?articleID=
8701482.

179   *UNICOR:* Check out UNICOR's service section, at www.unicor
.gov/services/.

181   *Interactive Voice Response:* IVR gets a whopping 1,500,000 Google
hits; voice-mail hell gets a few more, with 1,580,000.

183   *American Customer Satisfaction Index:* The ACSI survey data is
available online at www.theacsi.org/.

184   *new consumer apartheid:* See Diane Brady, "Why Service Stinks," *BusinessWeek,* October 23, 2000.

CHAPTER NINE

187   *Project for Excellence in Journalism:* This group, affiliated with the J-school at Columbia, is online at journalism.org. Their report, *The State of the News Media 2004,* is available online at www.stateofthenewsmedia.org/index.asp.

188   *decline in hard news:* See Thomas E. Patterson at the Joan Shorenstein Center on the Press, Politics and Public Policy, at Harvard, *Doing Well and Doing Good: How Soft News and Critical Journalism Are Shrinking the News Audience and Weakening Democracy—and What News Outlets Can Do About It.* The Center has a lot of research available online at www.ksg.harvard.edu/presspol/index.htm.

189   *Pew Research Center:* The Pew Research Center for the People and the Press conducts regular surveys on the news media. Surveys from the last five years are available online at people-press.org/reports/index.php?TopicID=1.

191   *Ben Bagdikian:* Bagdikian has been studying media consolidation since the early eighties, and his latest book is *The New Media Monopoly* (Beacon Press, 2004). He has a website as well, www.benbagdikian.com/.

191   *entertainment as news:* See *Changing Definitions of News,* a March 1998 study by the Committee of Concerned Journalists, available online at the journalism.org website, at www.journalism.org/resources/research/reports/definitions/default.asp.

193   *September 11:* See two Pew Center surveys for the rise and fall in public trust after 9-11: "Terror Coverage Boosts News Media's Image," November 2001, and "Public's News Habits Little Changed by September 11," July 2002.

195   *Bush press conference:* Video and text of the April 13, 2004, prime-time press conference is online at www.whitehouse.gov/news/releases/2004/04/20040413–20.html.

196   *Jeff Gannon:* See Howard Kurtz, "Jeff Gannon Admits Past Mistakes, Berates Critics," *Washington Post,* February 19, 2005, and the Gannongate links at the Media Matters for America website, at mediamatters.org/topics/gannongate.html.

199   *fairness doctrine:* There is a good capsule history of the fairness
      doctrine at the Museum of Broadcasting and Communications
      website, at www.museum.tv/archives/etv/F/htmlF/fairnessdoct/
      fairnessdoct.htm.

201   *James Fallows:* See "Why America Hates the Media," by Fallows, in
      the February 1996 issue of *The Atlantic Monthly.*

204   *Rathergate:* See www.rathergate.com/ for links to anti-Rather
      bloggers.

206   *less than a quarter:* See the Pew Research Center's "Public's News
      Habits Little Changed by September 11," cited above, particularly
      the section on the aging news audience.

206   *New York Times Magazine:* See Marshall Sella, "The Stiff Guy vs.
      The Dumb Guy," September 24, 2000, for more on the young
      getting their news from late-night TV.

209   *Online NewsHour forum:* The posting from the March 2002
      feature on youth and the news is still available online at
      www.pbs.org/newshour/forum/march02/news5.html.

CHAPTER TEN

212   *New York Times Magazine:* See Ron Suskind, "Without a Doubt:
      Faith, Certainty, and the Presidency of George W. Bush," October
      17, 2004.

214   *Garry Wills:* See "The Day the Enlightenment Went Out," *The
      New York Times,* November 4, 2004.

217   *ACTA:* ACTA reports are available at their website,
      www.goacta.org.

219   *Academic Bill of Rights:* David Horowitz writes about his bill in
      The Chronicle of Higher Education, February 13, 2004, in an
      article called "In Defense of Intellectual Diversity."

219   *Stanley Fish:* Professor Fish responds in the same issue of *The
      Chronicle of Higher Education,* in an article called "'Intellectual
      Diversity': Trojan Horse of a Dark Design."

Index

Dow Chemical, 6–7
downcoding, 149
Doyle, John, 197
Drexel Burnham Lambert, 159–60
Dukakis, Michael, 105

Eberle, Bernard, 196
economy:
  bubble bust, 42–44
  debt, 52–53, 62, 85
  double-income households, 49
  government subsidies, 16–17
  income inequality, 45–46, 57,
    59–65, 91
  labor unions, 56, 63–64
  long boom, 12–13, 46–53, 60
  manufacturing sector, 17, 47,
    57–58, 60
  market-driven, 13, 15–17,
    89–90
  money in, 16, 48, 49–50
  mutual funds, 50–52
  outsourced jobs, 56–57, 86,
    172, 177, 180
  poverty, 43, 216
  productivity, 58, 61
  service sector, 17, 47, 58, 60, 63
  speculation, 53, 56
  statistics, 59–60
  tax policies, 43, 61, 64, 85, 91,
    94, 103
  underemployment, 59–60
  unemployment, 17, 43, 55–59
  and war, 215
  wealth concentration, 46, 64
education, 33, 216–21
Enron, 6, 9, 17, 54, 67, 68, 72, 73,
  74, 86, 97, 101
escalation, 182
euphemisms, 1–3
Executive Life, 158–60

Fallows, James, 201
Federal Election Commission
  (FEC), 105–6
Fish, Stanley, 219
Fleischer, Ari, 2
Flynn, John, 33
Ford, Henry, 185
Fox News, 189, 197–98, 200, 204,
  206, 207
Frankfurt, Harry, 5
Franklin, Benjamin, 142
Freud, Sigmund, 32–33

Gannon, Jeff, 196–97
Gates, Bill, 47–48, 81
Gates, Bruce, 99
General Electric (GE), 56–57, 58,
  83, 86, 200
Gingrich, Newt, 8, 94, 96, 100,
  101, 102, 109
Global Crossing, 17, 69
Gore, Al, 7, 11
government:
  purpose of, 110
  social contract in, 95
Gramm, Phil, 74
Gramm-Leach-Bliley Financial
  Services Modernization Act,
  157–58

health insurance, 145, 146, 149–58
HealthSouth, 69, 73
Hearst, William Randolph, 198
Hefley, Joel, 98
Helms, Jesse, 105
Hicks, Bill, 24, 27
Hollinger International, 70
Holocaust, 219
Home Depot, 163, 165, 174
Horowitz, David, 219
hyperbole, 11–12

LAURA PENNY is thirty and tired of being put on hold. A teaching fellow at the University of King's College, she lives in Halifax, Nova Scotia.